Critical Acclaim for

The Magic of Encouragement

"Nothing is more important to a child's future than his own sense of self-worth. Stephanie Marston's lively guide for parents offers the kind of warm, practical advice that will transform relationships."

—Kenneth Blanchard, Ph.D.,
co-author of *The One Minute Manager*

"Any parent could benefit from reading this truly exciting book. Hardly a page without good, practical suggestions for improving one's parenting."

—Louise Bates Ames, Ph.D.,
associate director, Gesell Institute

"This book is a treasure! Rarely does a book entertain, educate, inspire, and motivate as much as this one does. It contains more wisdom and insight about building high self-esteem in children than any other book I have read."

—Jack Canfield, member, California Task Force
to Promote Self-Esteem and Social Responsibility,
and author of *100 Ways to Enhance Self-Concept in the Classroom*

"I learned some new tricks from this book. . . . worthwhile reading. . . . really good . . ."

—Marilyn Heins, M.D.,
Tucson Parent

"Written by a psychologist already distinguished for her parenting seminars and audiocassettes, *THE MAGIC OF ENCOURAGEMENT* offers clear, specific tools for raising children with self-esteem."

—*ALA Booklist*

Stephanie Marston has a master's degree in counseling psychology and is president of Raising Miracles Educational Seminars. She is also the mother of a fourteen-year-old daughter. She lives in Pacific Palisades, California.

D0168242

The Magic of Encouragement

Nurturing Your Child's Self-Esteem

STEPHANIE MARSTON

POCKET BOOKS

New York   London   Toronto   Sydney   Tokyo   Singapore

POCKET BOOKS, a division of Simon & Schuster Inc.
1230 Avenue of the Americas, New York, NY 10020

Marston, Stephanie.
   The magic of encouragement: nurturing your child's self-esteem /
Stephanie Marston.
     p. cm.
   Reprint. Originally published: New York : W. Morrow, c1990.
   Includes bibliographical references and index.
   ISBN: 0-671-73273-0 : $9.00
   1. Child rearing—United States. 2. Self-respect in children.
I. Title.
HQ769.M299   1992
649'.1—dc20   91-34234
                                      CIP

First Pocket Books trade paperback printing February 1992

10 9 8 7 6 5 4 3

POCKET and colophon are registered trademarks of
Simon & Schuster Inc.

Printed in the U.S.A.

To my friend and mentor Virginia Satir, who inspired me to discover the joy and fulfillment in valuing and accepting oneself.

and

To Beatrice Cooper, who has been a tremendous catalyst for change and growth in my life through her unconditional acceptance and loving guidance.

ACKNOWLEDGMENTS

Nothing occurs in a vacuum, and this book couldn't have been written without the participation of over a thousand parents who attended my seminars and were clients in my private practice. I am grateful to each and every one of them for so openly sharing their struggles, challenges, and successes with me.

I am deeply grateful to a number of people who have generously given me their support, guidance, and encouragement. All of us need a cheering squad rooting us on, especially in such a long and challenging project.

I wish to thank my daughter, Ama, for all that she has taught me about being a parent and for being my guinea pig and allowing me to practice on her. I am also appreciative of the continual opportunities she provides for me to re-parent myself.

Dr. and Mrs. Leon Small, my parents, have provided ongoing love, support, and encouragement throughout my life, and especially in this process. I also wish to thank them for giving me an independent spirit and determination and for always being there to help.

My editor, Liza Dawson, at William Morrow has been extremely enthusiastic throughout this project and has made the process a pleasure. Working with her has been a truly affirming experience.

I feel fortunate to be working with Patty Leasure, my literary agent. She has been supportive, optimistic, and encouraging. Her wholehearted belief in this project has been invaluable.

ACKNOWLEDGMENTS

Working with Celeste Fremon has been a true privilege. Her sensitivity, clarity, and responsiveness helped me to clarify and articulate my ideas, and I have grown as a writer through working with her.

A guiding light throughout my life has been Dorothy Kraft. She recognized my potential as a child, and through her warmth and sensitivity she encouraged me to express my creativity.

To my friends: Georgia Noble for her empathetic ear and eternal patience; Cathy and Dan Warren for their enthusiasm and their front-porch chats; Jordan Buck for her fervent support; Laurie Sale for her generosity and good business sense; Maureen Murdock for sharing her writer's perspective; Anne Parker for holding a thread of my history; Carol Trussel for reading the manuscript and giving me her valuable feedback and encouragement; and Ellen Fleischmann, who acted as a midwife in giving birth to my audiocassette program.

I am deeply indebted to the following people who have so generously given of their time and expertise as I developed my private practice and seminars.

Dr. Susan Brown, clinical director of the Julia Ann Singer Center, generously contributed her expertise and insights into family therapy, and was continually available over the years for consultation as I shifted the focus of my work to a family orientation.

Jack Canfield, president of Self-Esteem Seminars and president and founder of the Foundation for Self-Esteem, introduced me to the field of holistic education and inspired me to offer workshops to teachers and school administrators.

John Vasconcellos, California legislator and founder of the California Task Force to Promote Self-Esteem and Personal and Social Responsibility, shared with me the tenacity of his vision and supported my own work.

Ellen Galinsky and Susan Ginsburg at Bank Street College of Education supported and encouraged me in developing and implementing my corporate parenting seminars.

There are numerous people who have made it possible for

ACKNOWLEDGMENTS

me to present my seminars to the general public, and in corporations. In particular I would like to thank Judy Brunk, Deborah Bogan, and the staff and families at Hill an' Dale Family Learning Center for providing a nurturing environment in which to develop my seminars; Carolyn McCullough, Yolie Aguilar, and Sophia Speth at the Los Angeles Department of Water and Power; and Scott Peterson at ARCO.

CONTENTS

Throughout this book I use case studies from my seminars and clinical practice. I have changed all the names of the parents and children and anything that might identify them to protect their privacy.

S.M.

INTRODUCTION

"The point is not to do remarkable things, but to do ordinary things with the conviction of their immense importance."
—Teilhard de Chardin

Eleven years ago my life seemed like one continuous battle. I had always imagined myself as a loving, understanding parent, yet when I was faced with the everyday demands of parenting, my idea of myself as the all-nurturing earth mother deteriorated into my worst nightmare. I realized that I was totally unprepared for the reality of coping with a strong-willed, active child. My daughter was three years old at the time, and from morning to night it seemed I was constantly screaming, threatening, and nagging her. I fought every morning to get her dressed, sometimes for as much as forty-five minutes, during which time she continually talked back to me and frequently screamed, "I hate you!"

Bedtime was even worse. I would spend two hours getting her to bed every night, sitting in her room until she fell asleep and then creeping out of the room, while quite literally holding my breath and praying she wouldn't be awakened by the creaking floorboards. There were some nights when she would somehow hear my tiptoed retreat and wake up. I would then have to go through the entire tedious routine again. I felt I was being held hostage by my own child. And yet as frustrated as I was, I couldn't seem to change the situation.

Each night I would promise myself that tomorrow would be different. Yet each morning I found myself doing the very things I had vowed never to do or say and feeling guilty all over again. I was helpless, out of control, and embarrassed that this little person was able to disarm me so completely.

Not only was my daughter receiving the brunt of my wrath, but my husband also became the target of my frustration and rage. Our home was fast becoming a war zone. What was even more upsetting was that, at the time, I was consulting with teachers in how to enhance self-esteem in children and facilitating personal-growth workshops. Yet here I was unable to apply the most basic of these concepts and principles in my own family. I didn't understand why it was so easy for me to be patient and understanding with other children, while with my own daughter I so easily lost control.

One day the truth of the situation was presented to me in a way I could no longer ignore: I walked into the kitchen to find Ama cowering in the corner, her arms protectively over her face. Horrified, I asked what she was afraid of. "You're gonna hit me, Mommy, when you see the mess I made!"

I left the kitchen in a daze. How could things have progressed to such a point where my own child reacted to me with such terror? I resolved, in that moment, to find a better way to mold Ama's behavior. The problem was, how?

Over the years I had read numerous books on child development, parenting, and psychology. I knew that yelling, name-calling, threats, and spanking were all negative ways of changing children's behavior, and were consequently damaging to their self-esteem, but none of that knowledge seemed to help when I was in the midst of the struggle with my own daughter.

I could no longer ignore that all of my love and good intentions weren't enough to change my daughter's behavior—and regulate my own. At this point I became intrigued with the work of the late world-renowned family therapist Virginia Satir.

In 1950 Satir had pioneered the concept of family therapy. Up until then patients were only seen in individual sessions, and never from the perspective of how one person's issues and reactions affected the entire family's dynamics. In the following years her therapeutic approach revolutionized the entire field of psychotherapy, and more recently has become a new standard for therapeutic treatment.

I had read several of Satir's books, and become convinced that her approach held some vital keys to the issues with which I was struggling. (Virginia Satir's eight books have been translated into twenty-two different languages.)

I decided to study with her, and began a mentor relationship that would play a major role in my life for the next ten years.

As I studied, I was also applying the skills I was learning in my own home, and I began to experience dramatic changes in my family. Over time the yelling, threatening, and name-calling decreased as I found new ways of relating with my daughter. I felt more in charge, and she seemed responsive to my more humane approach. Most importantly, I began to feel better about myself as a parent.

Shortly after beginning my work with Virginia Satir, I entered a graduate program in child development, family therapy, communication skills, and self-esteem, and subsequently received a Master's degree in counseling psychology.

On becoming a psychotherapist, I realized it was time to do my own research into the qualities and characteristics of nurturing families. In the course of seeing hundreds of children in my clinical practice, I discovered some interesting things: I found that children are tremendously strong and resourceful, and will adapt to the unconscious and conscious messages and needs of their parents. I also confirmed for myself that in order for children to thrive psychologically, the entire family needs to be involved in the therapeutic process. It was at this juncture that I shifted my focus to counseling families and parents as well as children.

Over an eight-year period of working with hundreds of families, it became clear to me that self-esteem and communication were at the core of most family problems. It was at this point that I started to create an educational curriculum that would give parents the tools to establish a nurturing home atmosphere. Over the next several years I developed a series of workshops that I call Parenting for High Self-Esteem. In doing so, I discovered that although parents clearly intended to communicate lovingly with their kids, their actions often had a negative effect. My goal was to help parents to find ways to transmit their love and caring so that they could mold their children's behavior, and see that their children felt good about themselves in the process.

In every one of my seminars parents inevitably ask the same questions: How do I get my child dressed in the morning as I'm rushing to get to work? What do I do when my kids won't put their toys or clothes away? How can I encourage my child to talk to me? Why do I feel so guilty about being away from my kids? What can I do when my child gives up too easily when he's learning a new skill? How do I get my child to listen to me? What can I do to comfort my daughter when she is upset?

Unfortunately parents know what they *don't* want to do. But they are usually unsure of what they should do instead and the shift to a more positive parenting approach is perplexing to most parents.

In my seminars I provide parents not so much with specific answers as with a road map to help them navigate through the unfamiliar territory of parenthood. During the course of a six-week series, I teach them how to encourage cooperation and to avoid daily power struggles, how to recognize and acknowledge their children's feelings, how to set clear, firm limits on behavior while fostering independence and responsibility, how to enhance their children's sense of competence and confidence, how to express their anger constructively and bypass the negative effects of criticism, and last but very definitely not least, how to enhance their own self-esteem in the process of raising their children.

In each session I introduce a new technique, allowing time for guided practice through the use of role-playing and group discussions. There is a question-and-answer period at the end of each session, and parents are given homework assignments in order to let them practice what they learned in class. The following week they return, and we discuss and refine their skills as well as debug any problems they may have encountered. This allows them to refine their newly acquired skills while gaining confidence.

Time and time again parents would return to my classes excited, reporting how the new tools and skills they had learned had dramatically changed their relationships with their kids. It was a result of this consistently positive feedback that I decided to write this book.

PARENTS AS ARCHITECTS OF THE FAMILY

We are responsible for designing the blueprints upon which our families will be built. As you think about your family, ask yourself, "What kind of person do I want my child to become?" and "What can I do to make this happen?" From the answers to these two questions you will develop your blueprint.

When I ask this question in my seminars, the list of qualities that come back from parents are usually very similar: "I want my children to be self-reliant, responsible, compassionate, loving, trustworthy, creative, enthusiastic, self-confident, honest, capable, positive, and able to stand on their own two feet. . . ." In Yiddish the word for such a person is *mensch*. Mensches are people who conduct their life with strength, compassion, and dignity. Our families are the context in which such a person develops.

Many of us are being asked to teach our children things we never learned ourselves. For example, I *realized* the importance of structure and effective discipline in parenting, yet I didn't have a clue about how to go about instituting effective discipline. I found it difficult to control my own temper, much less help my child to monitor hers. (There's nothing like having kids to show us the gaps in our learning.) Many times I have felt I was barely one step ahead of what I was teaching my child, but my commitment to learn and grow propelled me to improve my understanding and skills.

My hope is that as you read this book, you will begin to have some insights about what *is* working in your family and, conversely, will find the support to change those things that *aren't* working quite as well as you'd like them to.

PUT YOUR WHIP AWAY

A cautionary note: We've all heard the phrase "Hindsight is 20/20 vision." There is no point in using your new insight to blame yourself for past mistakes. Blaming yourself is not only a waste of energy, it interferes with change and new learning. It's never too late to improve your parenting skills. However, learning and integrating new skills is a process that takes time, patience, and practice. But remember if these new tools work even 10 percent of the time, that 10 percent will still have a big impact on the other 90 percent of your relationship with your kids.

HOW TO USE THIS BOOK

"Before I got married I had six theories about bringing up children; now I have six children and no theories."
John Wilmot, *Earl of Rochester*

There are no hard and fast rules for raising children, but there are guidelines that can be modified to match the needs of each parent and each child. Although there is no one right way to approach a situation, my hope is that I can help you to cultivate a bag of tricks that will provide you with choices in handling your everyday parenting challenges differently.

My friend Virginia Satir used to say, "Taste everything, but swallow only that which fits." In other words, I hope that you will be open to the concepts and techniques I offer you, but if you find that one technique I suggest doesn't work with your particular situation, let it go and try the next approach.

To improve our relationship with our kids, we don't have to grow another arm or make a million dollars. We only need to change our attitudes and learn new skills. Effective parenting doesn't require anything you don't already have. You simply need to become acquainted with your existing resources and learn how to use them.

Just as Michelangelo saw the "David" in the raw, unformed block of marble before he struck it with his chisel, we as parents can imagine the fine adult human beings who will emerge from our children's growing, evolving selves. By holding this image in our minds, we can, through our encouragement, nurture our children to blossom into their fullest potential.

Chapter 1
THE BEST GIFT YOU CAN GIVE YOUR CHILDREN

"We all become more beautiful when we are loved, and if you have self-love, then you are always beautiful."
—Alice Walker, *The Color Purple*

Not long ago a friend of mine had a baby. As I stared into the window at the rows of infants laying in their bassinets, I was struck with how similar they looked. Yes, some had dark hair, some curly hair, and some had no hair at all. Some were larger or weighed a bit more than others, but mostly they were all pretty much equal. What would happen, I asked myself, if the babies come back thirty-five years later for a reunion? What would we find?

Both research and common sense tell us that we'd find that some people took life by its tail and made the most of it. Some would be successes in business or art. Others would be exceptional parents, teachers, lawyers, nurses, etc. Statistics also tell us that we'd find others whose futures had taken quite a divergent turn. Some would have addictions to drugs or alcohol. Others would somehow just be unable to make their lives work. And there would even be a couple of those children who wouldn't be there at all. They are the ones who would have decided to take their own lives as a result of their pain, despair, and inability to cope with life at even its most basic level.

I started to think about what caused these incredibly varied outcomes: How could all these children who started out so equal have ended up so differently? Oh, I suppose some of the discrepancy could be attributed to genetics, but what about the rest? Did a fairy fly through the room with magic dust and sprinkle some but not others? No, not unless reality was created by Walt Disney. In the last twelve years of my working with people, I've discovered that the single most important factor that determines whether children grow up to be happy and successful is their self-esteem. Self-esteem is the *real* magic wand that can form a child's future. A child's self-esteem affects every area of her existence, from the friends she chooses, to how well she does academically in school, to what kind of job she gets, to even the person she chooses to marry. But what exactly is this elusive, intangible thing called self-esteem?

WHAT IS SELF-ESTEEM?

Defined simply, self-esteem is the sense of being *lovable* and *capable*. When these two qualities are in sync, a child has high self-esteem. Children need first to know that they are loved and accepted for who they are. Then, with this as a basis, their natural impulse is to take that love and learn to contribute it to the world in constructive ways. It's not hard to see that self-esteem is the best gift you can give your children. And as you work to give your child this marvelous gift, the most important thing to understand is this: *Self-esteem evolves in kids primarily through the quality of our relationships with them.* Because they can't see themselves directly, children know themselves by reflection. For the first several years of their lives, you are their major influence. Later on, teachers and friends come into the picture. But especially at the beginning, you're it with a capital *I*.

WE ARE GODS TO OUR KIDS

Because children see parents as authority figures and gods, they think that the way you treat them is the way they deserve to be treated: "What you say about me is what I am" is a literal truth to your child. Consequently, when children are treated with respect, they conclude that they deserve respect and hence develop *self*-respect. When children are treated with acceptance, they develop self-acceptance; when they are cherished, they conclude that they deserve to be loved, and they develop self-esteem. Conversely, if they are mistreated or abused, they conclude that they deserve that, too.

Parents are, in effect, mirrors: What we reflect back to our kids becomes the basis for their self-image, which in turn influences all areas of their lives. To put it another way, who our children are is not nearly as important as who they *think* they are.

THE HIGH COST OF LOW SELF-ESTEEM

I hardly need to tell you that the American family is in a period of crisis. Every day in America 1,375 teenagers drop out of school! In 1986, 1.4 million teens became pregnant. That means that every day twelve hundred teenagers have babies, and fourteen adolescents per day become pregnant with their *third* child.[1] Teen suicide has tripled over the last twenty years in this country, and according to the National Center for Health's study, every seventy-eight seconds an adolescent attempts suicide. Drugs are threatening the lives of our children from affluent suburban families to their less well-off inner-city counterparts. There are almost 2 million teenagers currently using illicit drugs, and a significant percentage begin at ages nine and ten.[2] When we confront these disturbing statistics, it becomes all too evident that all the love in the world is not always enough to help kids cope with the daily challenges of life. There is another essential aspect of parenting that requires more than love. It requires recognition of how our words and actions affect the formation of our children's self-esteem.

YOUR CHILD'S OWN VCR

Imagine that between your child's eyes and ears is a videocassette recorder. Everything our children hear, see, and feel is recorded onto a cassette. Guess who is the big star in their movie? You are. What you say and, more important, what you do, is recorded there for them to replay over and over again. We all have videocassettes. Adults just have larger libraries of tapes available.

In the course of this book I'll take you through a step-by-step process that will teach you how you can create positive images on these cassettes, and give you practical tools for enhancing your children's feelings of being lovable and capable.

The first of those steps is to gain a greater understanding of the nature of self-esteem itself.

ON TOP OF THE WORLD

Take a moment and recall a time when you felt really good about yourself. What were you doing? Whom were you with? Remember the experience in as much detail as possible. Think about what contributed to your feeling so good. Most likely it can be described by one or more of the following feelings:

- You felt that you were important to someone whom you respected and whose opinion you valued.
- You felt you did something that only you could have done in that particular way. You felt special and had a sense of your own unique gifts.

- You felt you were in charge and getting the things done that you set out to do. You felt confident that you could handle whatever you were faced with.
- You shared a difficult-to-express thought, feeling, or opinion with someone, and in doing so, you connected with that person on a deeper level than ever before.

Each of the above feelings is representative of one of the four primary aspects of this ephemeral state called high self-esteem. If you look closely, you will observe that the experience you had satisfied a basic emotional need that in turn reinforced your belief in your value and competence as a person. Self-esteem is your ability to value yourself and to treat yourself with love, dignity, and respect. When we experience high self-esteem, we feel that the world is a better place because we are here. We radiate a sense of trust and hope. Integrity, honesty, love, and compassion flow freely from people who have high self-worth.[3]

FOUR FACTORS FOR HIGH SELF-ESTEEM

Self-esteem functions in precisely the same way in children: Only if their basic emotional needs are filled, can they learn to like and value themselves. For this reason understanding our children's needs is the first step in creating the proper climate for healthy growth and development. Our kids have lots and lots of individual needs, but they can all be grouped into four main categories.

Belonging
Uniqueness
Power
Freedom of Expression

When children experience a sense of satisfaction in each of these areas, self-esteem results.[4] These conditions are necessary no matter what the form of your family: single-parent family, blended family, intact family, same-sex-parent family.

I'll be exploring these four factors in greater detail in some of the following chapters. But let's begin with an overview of the basic concepts:

Belonging

Belonging is first on the list simply because children are social beings, and their most fundamental need is to feel connected. They develop a sense of security through feeling that they belong within a group. The most obvious group is, of course, your family. But as kids get older, they expand their need to belong to include outside groups as well, such as clubs, teams, their class, and the like. Most of what our kids do is geared toward finding "their place" in their families and in the world. In broad terms, a sense of belonging is developed through their relationships to people, places, and things. The primary way kids develop a sense of belonging is when they feel loved by someone who regards them as special. Moreover, they need to know that this someone will protect and guide them. Children also require a sense of history. They need to have a sense of their roots and heritage. Have you ever noticed that kids are fascinated by stories about what they were like when they were babies and what they said and did as they grew? This sense of history and connectedness increases your children's feelings of security and safety, and helps them build the ability to make healthy connections in the world at large.

Uniqueness

Over 5 billion people now live on this planet, and yet no two people have the same fingerprints. We all have some basic similarities with the rest of humanity, yet all of our kids are unique unto themselves. Very early on, our children discover that they are different from you and others in their lives and vice versa. However, parents often tend unconsciously to thwart this discovery by focusing on the similarities between themselves and their kids, and ignoring and/or rejecting the differences. Consequently you'll find that throughout this book I'll be stressing the importance of recognizing, accepting, and appreciating these differences we have with our kids. This requires that we see our children as *separate* in order to encourage their own unique development. Each child has his own individual expression to offer to the world. That expression can take many forms, from artistic interests, a way of thinking, athletic activities, a particular style of dressing, musical talents, different hobbies, etc. Our job is to join our children in discovering who they are.

Your child is a treasure, a human miracle, rare and irreplaceable. When you recognize and honor this truth, you relate to your kids more as individuals, and thus enhance their self-esteem.

Power

A sense of power is essential for every human being. For our children to have a strong sense of power, they need to feel that they can influence their environment and have some control over their lives. In order to accomplish this, they require our help in learning how to use their skills and abilities to positively impact their circumstances. They also need to know that they can make good decisions and solve problems. By allowing our kids to make decisions for themselves and solve their own problems, we help them to develop a sense of independence and personal power.

It is additionally empowering for children to feel that they can make meaningful contributions to their families. When we give them responsibility, it is a vote of confidence in their developing sense of competence. Empowerment is also gained when children see that they can accomplish what they set out to do. There is a tremendous power in mastering any new task. But mastery is a learned process, so our kids need our support and encouragement in learning new skills and achieving their goals. Every time they accomplish a task, their belief in themselves and in their ability increases manyfold.

The Five Freedoms
By Virginia Satir[5]

The freedom to see and hear what is here instead of what should be, was, or will be.

The freedom to say what one feels and thinks, instead of what one should.

The freedom to feel what one feels, instead of what one ought.

The freedom to ask for what one wants, instead of always waiting for permission.

The freedom to take risks in one's own behalf, instead of choosing to be only "secure" and not rocking the boat.

Freedom of Expression

Every family should extend First Amendment rights to all its members, but this freedom is particularly essential for our kids. Children must be able to say what they think, openly express their feelings, and ask for what they want and need if they are ever to develop an integrated sense of self. They must be able to think their own thoughts, even if they differ from ours. They need to have the opportunity to ask us questions when they don't understand what we mean. When our children grow up in an atmosphere where this kind of freedom is fostered and encouraged, there is room for them to grow as individuals, to engage in open, honest dialogues with us, and to realize the richness of their inner resources.

Needless to say, although kids blossom in a home atmosphere in which they can ask for what they want, they must also recognize that they may not always *get* what they've asked for. But they should never be blamed for asking.

I've noticed over the years that kids who are allowed to be emotionally honest develop a genuineness that more repressed kids don't ever seem to acquire. Their words match their facial expressions. Their actions match their words, and they relate from a position of strength.

If I were to give two guiding principles to help you understand your kids—their actions and their motivation—the first would be to get to know your kids' needs, and to examine how they are currently being met in the four areas we've just discussed.

Belonging, uniqueness, power, and freedom of expression are all essential for the health and well-being of every single child, regardless of age. If one or more of these conditions is lacking, it will impair a child's self-esteem from fully developing.

The second principle to remember is this: *Our kids are always trying to get their needs met.* Consequently, if one of these four basic needs is unfulfilled, the child will focus a great deal of his attention on that area in order to fill the emotional hole the best way he can.

To give you a better idea of how this works, I'd like you to meet three kids who, when I first got to know them, were *not* having their needs fully met.

PORTRAITS OF LOW SELF-ESTEEM

"If I were to search for the central core of difficulty in people as I have come to know them, it is that in the great majority of cases they despise themselves, regarding themselves as worthless and unloveable."
—Dr. Carl Rogers

Steven is four years old and lives in a very busy family. Both his parents work at high-powered jobs. He has a younger sister who has just turned two. If you could peek into Steven's life, this is what you would see:

Steven's father wakes him up and says, "Come on slowpoke, get a move on it, or you'll be late for school." Steven gets dressed, walks into the kitchen, and sits down at the table, ready for breakfast. His father and sister are already eating their cereal when he begins chattering away, "Did you see *Sesame Street* yesterday? Big Bird was taking all the kids to the fire· house. I love Big Bird, but really my favorite person is Oscar. He's so grumpy all the time. . . ." Steven continues babbling, trying to gets his parents' attention, until his father finally yells, "Steven, please! I don't care about Big Bird! Just eat your breakfast, or you'll be late for school." Steven grows quiet and finishes only part of his food.

Steven arrives at preschool and runs into the the block area along with several other boys. They dump the containers full of wooden blocks onto the tile floor. Larry claims an area, announcing, "I'm gonna make a block city!," and begins busily building his project, complete with skyscrapers, bridges, and parking garages. Steven plays nearby with some cars. He looks up and sees Larry's city, and yells, "Look out, earthquake!" He then proceeds to ram his car into the blocks, which come crashing down onto the floor. Larry's city is completely destroyed. He glares at Steven and screams, "You wrecked my city! I hate you! I don't want to play with you anymore."

Just then a teacher comes over and asks, "What happened here?" "Steven ruined my city," Larry says tearfully. "He drove his car into it and wrecked it." Steven jumps up and starts slugging Larry before the teacher can intervene. "Steven, no hitting," she says, physically restraining him. "You'd better come with me if you can't play considerately around the other kids." Steven is removed from the block area and is sent over to circle time with Ruth.

Ruth invites him into the circle, gives him a rug square to sit on, and asks, "Steven, would you like to tell us what you did over the weekend?" "No," Steven answers angrily. "I didn't do anything. You can't make me talk." "You're right, Steven," Ruth replies, recognizing how angry he is feeling. "You don't have to talk. That's fine."

As she begins to read a story to the group, she glances up and notices that Steven is pushing and pinching the kids on either side of him. "Steven," she sighs, "Please come and sit up here next to me. I see you're having a hard time keeping your hands to yourself." He crawls along the floor, while Ruth continues reading. As he is sitting next to her, he starts sticking out his tongue and making faces at the other kids, and distracts their attention away from the story. Ruth finally gives up and takes him over to the "time out" chair. "I want you to sit here and think about what you did," she says. "When you can control yourself, come back and join the circle."

It is clear that Steven is crying out for several things. He wants attention and to feel connected. But because he doesn't feel good about himself, he continually finds aggressive, disruptive ways of getting these needs met.

If you could listen to Steven's internal dialogue about himself, it would probably sound something like this; "I'm not very important. Nobody really likes me. Nobody wants to play with me. The kids think I'm dumb and too bossy. No one will pay attention to me. Even my parents don't like me." In short, he lacks several of the four factors for self-esteem. He certainly doesn't feel powerful. He doesn't feel his parents listen to and respect him, and his sense of belonging to his family is badly eroded. So he attempts to fill in these emotional voids in the only way he knows how. For example, when Steven ruined Larry's block city, he was begging his friends to notice him and to act scared of him so that he could think of himself as powerful.

All children strive to see themselves as strong and capable. But if they cannot, they will match their behavior to their self-images. A child who believes that he is bad shapes his actions to fit his view of himself. A lack in one or more of the four factors that make up self-esteem is the real cause of misbehavior. What usually happens is that the more a child misbehaves, the more he is punished, scolded, and rejected, the less his needs are met, and the more firmly established his belief that he is bad becomes. It's a vicious, destructive cycle.

Watch, for example, what happens when Elise, age nine, wakes up and goes downstairs for breakfast. As she is eating her eggs, she mutters, "I'm not going to school today. There's gonna be an awful test in English."

"Don't be ridiculous, young lady," her mother replies. "Now, get upstairs and get dressed!" Elise's worried feelings are ignored. Self-esteem slips a notch.

Elise grabs her lunch and runs out the door to meet her car pool. She piles into the backseat and begins talking with the three other girls, who always seem to be better friends with each other than with her.

When they arrive at school, Elise trips getting out of the car. "What a klutz," says one of the girls and the others giggle in response. The girls run into the school building laughing, as Elise lags behind at the curb. Her self-esteem has slipped yet another notch.

In class the day starts with an art project. While other students are busily working, Elise sits at her desk, frustrated, glue everywhere, staring into outer space. Just then her teacher walks over. "What's the matter, Elise?" inquires the teacher. "It looks like you've given up on your project."

"I can't make it look right!" Elise says, screwing up her face in a scowl. "It's just gross!" Her teacher tries to cajole her. "Come on now, don't be silly. It looks fine." But Elise only feels worse. "This is a dumb project anyway. I hate it."

Next Elise takes the dreaded English test and as she suspected, she does poorly: She barely passes with a 65. She stuffs her test into her desk, feeling discouraged, her sense of power and mastery in bad shape. At recess she goes outside to play kickball. As she walks into the yard, she sees that all her friends are standing together. She wants to be included so badly that she tries too hard with them. "Want a piece of my candy? I'll walk home with you after school. You can borrow my new blouse." Her overeager need to belong turns her friends off, and she experiences another rejection.

When Elise gets her report card, she hands it to her mother and flees the room. Her mother stares at the two "C"s and four "D"s, frowns, and follows Elise to the bedroom, where Elise is flopped on her bed. "Elise, this is a terrible report card! Why can't you be more like your sister? She does so well in school. I can't understand what's wrong with you."

At this point Elise's self-esteem is basically nonexistent. Her mother rolls her eyes to the ceiling. "Wait until your father comes home. We're going to have a long talk about this."

After dinner "the talk" takes place in the family room. Dad begins, "Your teacher says you haven't been handing in your homework, and you aren't making any effort in class. What do you have to say about this?" Elise is defensive. "It's not my fault Mrs. Peters doesn't like me and gives me bad grades no matter what I do. Besides, I didn't know I had to turn in all those assignments. She never told me." Before anything more can be said, Elise gets up and runs away in tears, yelling as she goes, "I'll never get good grades! It's not fair! Nothing I do is ever good enough."

With Steven and Elise, you can observe how their inability to satisfy their self-esteem needs has developed into a self-perpetuating cycle of defeat.

Let's see what happens when a child who has low self-esteem reaches adolescence.

Peter, fourteen, was very unsure of himself when he entered seventh grade. He was awkward and shy and considered a loner. On this particular day he comes home from school, puts a note on the kitchen table, and goes directly into his room. When his mother reads the note, she follows him. "Why were you sent to the opportunity room again today?" "I don't know," Peter grumbles sullenly. "That fat cow Ms. Williams said I was late for class again."

"Were you?"

That's Sondra, his mom, speaking. And again Peter ducks the issue. "Well, it wasn't my fault. I couldn't get my locker open." That's it for Sondra. "Peter, I just don't know what to do with you anymore!" she explodes. "At the rate you're going, you're never going to amount to anything." And she storms out. Sondra and her husband, Skip, are clueless as to how to handle their son's behavior. The more withdrawn and abusive he becomes, the more his parents avoid him.

Peter has developed a reputation at school of being a troublemaker. His grades are poor, and he avoids participating in class discussions, keeping his ideas and opinions to himself. He is regularly late for his classes, and is a frequent visitor to the office. He has few friends, and feels like an outsider with the friends he has. Like Steven and Elise, he has become stuck in a vicious cycle that is difficult to break. The worse his relationships with his family and friends are, the less he can concentrate on his schoolwork and . . . well, you get the picture. It doesn't matter how bright the child is; if his personal sense of capability is shot full of holes, he will do poorly. Such is the case with Peter.

The weekend after the blowup with his mom, Peter goes to the mall with his one friend, Brian, to hang out. His father receives a call from the store detective, who informs him that his son has been picked up for shoplifting. Skip is utterly beside himself when he goes to the store to pick up Peter. "What were you thinking when you stole that pocketknife?" Skip asks, his anger barely in check. Peter does his usual not-my-fault routine. "It wasn't my idea, Dad. Brian told me to do it. I didn't think we'd get caught." "You're grounded for a month, and that means no phone calls, either!" Skip shouts back in utter frustration. His father's threats of grounding fall on deaf ears. Peter just grows silent, refusing to show any emotion. It is the only protective stance he knows to avoid any further hurt or disappointment.

Obviously Peter is on a fast track to disaster if something doesn't change. He has a "D" average in school, and is in danger of being suspended because he has been sent to the office so many times. Moreover, Peter is so unsure of himself and wants to fit in with the guys so badly that he is very susceptible to peer pressure to acting out in negative ways.

STUCK ON THE MERRY-GO-ROUND OF LOW SELF-ESTEEM

Whenever a child sees himself as a loser and expects to fail, he will behave in a way that is bound to fulfill the prophesy. Once he stops believing in himself, he is on the road to failure. Peter, like Elise and Steven, felt that he was nothing in the eyes of his family, and that he didn't have what it took to fit in with his friends or to get good grades. He saw himself as bad, dumb, incompetent (i.e., lacking in power), and unlovable. He was withdrawn, filled with self-doubt, and absolutely unable to communicate his most pressing needs. The more he misbehaved and acted out, the more people punished and rejected him. And the more firmly entrenched he became in the belief that he was irretrievably "bad."

IS THERE HOPE FOR MY CHILD?

We can see that these kids are in trouble, but the real question is, what can be done about it *now*? At every seminar I teach, three or four parents inevitably approach me with that same question: "If my child has low self-esteem, is he ruined for life, or can his attitude be changed?" The answer is, of course, yes, attitudes can always be changed. Remember, self-esteem is learned, not something genetically inherited. And fortunately children are profoundly resilient and flexible. What they need immediately is frequent positive experiences with the important people in their lives. Even after a long string of negative experiences, children will almost always respond to an affirming atmosphere and positive reflections.

Steven is a perfect illustration. A little over six months ago the director of Steven's school called to let me know that she had given my name to his parents and suggested that they see me for some counseling. She described Steven as a sweet child, but starved for attention.

Several days later Nancy and Bob called, and we set up an evening appointment. When they came to see me, it was obvious that they were caring parents who were overwhelmed with the job of raising two small children and working full time.

"I never thought it would be this hard!" Nancy said, bursting into tears. "I know Steve is upset, but I just don't know what to do. I feel like all I ever do is yell at him or punish him. This sounds terrible, but some days I dread picking him up from school. He makes me so angry!"

Bob leaned over to comfort his wife as he added, "I know what you mean. He's so demanding. I just want some peace and quiet when I get home from the office, and he's all over me. I never thought raising kids would be like this!"

As you can see, both parents were feeling very insecure and helpless in relation to their son. "It's strange," Bob mused. "Here I am, a top executive, in charge of an office full of people, and I come home and this four-year-old makes me come unglued. I can't believe that I can't get this kid to behave!"

I reassured them that they were not alone in their struggles, and pointed out that raising kids takes a very specific set of skills, which most of us never learned. I went on to explain that once they were more in charge of the situation and felt better about themselves as parents, they would be able to relate with Steven in a way that was more satisfying for everyone.

When I observed Steven at school, I could tell that he was searching for a way to fit in and to feel accepted by the other kids. He acted overly anxious. Steven flitted from one activity to another; it was obviously difficult for him to concentrate on any task for more than a few minutes. He would run up to other children and try to gain their attention by pulling their hair or pinching. It wasn't surprising that his parents didn't want to be around him. Neither Nancy nor Bob felt proud of their parenting, and Steven, by his behavior, was continually pointing out their deficiencies and inadequacies.

As we began to work together, I explained what happens when a child feels like a "bad kid" and attempts to get his need for attention met. Because this need is so fundamental, Steven would rather have negative attention than no attention at all. As I was talking, a light went on for Bob. "So is that why he chatters incessantly at the breakfast table and constantly interrupts me?" Yes, I replied. Because Steven's babbling was so annoying, they would cut him off and reject him, which reinforced his feeling of insecurity and worthlessness. "What do we do?" Bob asked. "I can't take the constant noise." I explained that as Steven began to gain their attention in more positive ways, his need to chatter and distract them would decrease. I reminded them that *they* were in charge of shaping how he got his needs met. As long as Steven was feeling "bad," he would continue to find negative avenues of expression.

Nancy was puzzled. "What can we do to get Steven to stop hitting his little sister? He talks baby talk and wants me to treat him like a baby." I explained to them that frequently when a new brother or sister arrives on the scene, children regress to more infantile behaviors, such as talking baby talk, asking for a bottle, having sleep difficulties, or wetting the bed. This is a reaction to being dethroned and losing their place at the center of attention. I helped Steven's parents see that with understanding, special attention, and time these conditions would turn themselves around. Once Nancy and Bob understood the situation from Steven's perspective, they began to feel more compassionate toward their son, seeing him more as *a child with needs* rather than *a child with problems.*

I coached Nancy and Bob in how to acknowledge Steven's feelings while limiting his actions. I told them to use phrases like, "I bet you sometimes wish that you were still a baby"; "You're my special big boy, and no one can ever take your place"; "I know your little sister makes you mad sometimes. It's okay to feel mad, but it's not okay to hit her." It was obvious that Nancy was upset with Steven's need to be little again, but I reminded her that Steven, in his own way, was telling her that he wanted her focused time, attention, and nurturing. I suggested that she not be overly concerned with his desire to regress, but that both she and Bob should concentrate on spending time alone with him on a regular basis.

After several weeks Nancy and Bob started to feel more in charge, and Steven's behavior began to change. Nancy established a regular Tuesday afternoon date with her son, and Bob scheduled a couple of uninterrupted hours with him on the weekends. "He seems to eat it up!" reported Nancy. "One week I forgot, and he kept asking me when we would have our time. I can see how important it is to him." Bob added, "When I come home in the evening, I make a point of giving Steve a big hug and talking to him for a few minutes before I sit down to unwind. I can't believe it, but those few minutes seem to make such a difference. He's not so demanding after that. We've also started taking turns putting the kids to bed at night. Every night one of us goes in and does the bedtime ritual with each of the kids. This way they each get our focused time and attention. It seems to be working. Boy"—he grinned—"am I relieved."

During our next few meetings we discussed several new approaches that would help Steven feel more important and in charge of himself. Bob and Nancy agreed to encourage Steve to do small chores, such as folding napkins or helping put away the laundry. I explained that this would give him a feeling of significance as a contributing member of their family. I reminded them to make sure to acknowledge his efforts so he would feel recognized and appreciated.

After a month Steven still hit his sister, but only at moments of high frustration. He was doing much better at school, and had gone over a week without hitting other kids. He was visibly feeling more connected to his parents and was coping more maturely with his feelings of anger and jealousy. Nancy was actively teaching Steven how to use words when he felt angry or upset, and his teachers reinforced this.

After several months Steven had progressed dramatically. He now used his energy to build rather than to destroy. He was willing to try new things, confident of his ability to meet new challenges. He volunteered to do chores both at school and at home. He played cooperatively with other kids, and was frequently invited to play at their houses. At home he was more amenable and relaxed. His chattering and hitting had stopped completely. In short, he was becoming a child with self-esteem.

Now, what about Elise?

Like Nancy and Bob, Elise's parents were well-meaning, but lacked the necessary skills to create a more positive atmosphere for their daughter. Her mother's criticism and comparisons to her older sister only reinforced Elise's feelings of hopelessness and worthlessness. Elise was treated as though she were a problem child because her parents didn't recognize her despair, discouragement, and low self-esteem. They were unaware that her behavior was a desperate attempt at getting her basic needs met. Once they understood the underlying causes of her misbehavior, they were able to see Elise as a child who was discouraged and starved for attention, affection, and encouragement. As they focused more on her efforts and small improvements, building on her strengths, she started to feel better about herself.

In Elise's case it was necessary to teach her parents how to help her in creating structure and routines in her life. She needed a structure for doing her homework, including a particular place and a regular time that she could count on being "homework time." Because she felt so discouraged, I suggested that her parents break her study time down into smaller increments to allow her to feel successful in completing tasks.

When children feel powerless, their parents need to provide more positive feedback for them by focusing on their efforts and finding tasks at which they can be successful. With a change in atmosphere at home and parental support Elise gradually began to believe in herself. After working with the family for less than a year, her grades came up and, like Steven, when she felt a greater acceptance at home, her peer relationships improved tremendously.

And what about Peter? Peter was the hardest. Because of his age, his self-destructive patterns were more ingrained than with the two younger children. Worse yet, Peter's parents had given up on him. They had withdrawn from him and adopted the attitude "He's too much to handle. He's on his own." With these complexities in mind I recommended that he do both individual counseling as well as get involved in an adolescent support group. Then I worked with his parents in setting up a structure with clearly defined rules, consequences, and rewards. It was necessary to help them understand that although Peter acted apathetic and tough, it was a cover-up to hide his feelings of inadequacy and insecurity. Like Steven and Elise, what he really needed was his parents' loving involvement, encouragement, and effective discipline. Sondra and Skip sat down with Peter and devised a system of rules and consequences as well as a structure for doing homework. Peter began to have his teachers sign a sheet indicating whether he handed in his homework on time. At the end of the week he would show the chart to his parents, and Sondra and Skip focused on Peter's effort and improvement, no matter how slight. When Peter returned home from school with a fully starred assignment sheet, both Sondra and Skip let Peter know how happy they were with his achievement.

And as with Steven and Elise, the work paid off. Peter is no longer a "lost cause." He is doing better in school, maintaining a solid "C" average. Peter joined the junior-varsity soccer team and began developing new friendships through his involvement with the team. He's been earning extra money by doing chores for neighbors. When he's earned enough, his parents have promised to match his savings so he can buy a set of roller blades, since Peter has developed a new passion for sports.

When you make a conscious choice to insure that your kid's needs for belonging, uniqueness, power, and expression are truly being met, you will find some amazing changes occurring in a relatively short time. It's never too late to start. Don't think for a minute that because your children are already teenagers, it's too late. That's simply not true. It's never too late to help change their self-image and to change the dynamics of the family.

When children feel good about themselves, it's like a snow-ball rolling downhill. They are continually able to recognize and integrate new proof of their value as they grow and mature. They come to understand that they are in a process of developing and have realistic expectations of their capabilities, knowing that these capabilities will increase. And they are open to trying new experiences and taking the risks necessary to learn new skills.

Children with high self-esteem radiate an inner sense of security that is reflected in their actions. They are able to freely express their thoughts, opinions, and feelings, and can constructively work at solving problems.

The following two lists will give you an easy thumbnail reference that lets you assess the state of a child's self-esteem.

A child with high self-esteem:
- is proud of his or her accomplishments.
- can act independently.
- assumes responsibility.
- can tolerate frustration.
- approaches challenges with enthusiasm.
- feels capable of taking charge of situations in his or her own life.
- has a good sense of humor.
- has a sense of purpose.

- can postpone gratification.
- seeks help when needed.
- is confident and resourceful.
- is active, energetic and spontaneously expresses his or her feelings.
- is relaxed and can manage stress.

A child with low self-esteem:
- plays it safe by avoiding situations that require taking risks.
- feels powerless.
- becomes easily frustrated.
- is overly sensitive.
- constantly needs reassurance.
- is easily influenced by others.
- frequently uses the phrases "I don't know" or "I don't care."
- is withdrawn.
- blames others for his failures.
- is isolated, has few friends, is preoccupied.
- is uncooperative, angry.
- is uncommunicative.
- is clingy, dependent.
- is constantly complaining.
- has a general negative attitude.[6]

Ask yourself, What kind of self-esteem am I building in my children and reinforcing in me? Spend time observing your children's behavior, and you will learn a lot about their internal self-image. We can read the clues in our children in the same way we learn to read a road map. Watch and notice how they handle conflict, disappointment, and failure. Do they attempt to get their needs met directly? Do they take risks and try out new activities? Do they express their thoughts, feelings, and opinions openly? What are their peer relationships like? How do they handle rejection and competition? By observing these coping strategies, you will learn a lot about how your child feels about himself.

Go over both lists and check off the characteristics that apply to your child. You will begin to see a pattern. If most of your checks are on the high self-esteem list, then you know your child is in good shape. Congratulations. You're ahead of the game. If you check five or more on the low self-esteem list, then you have some work ahead of you. And that's okay. The principles you'll learn in the course of reading this book, combined with your concern and desire, will enable you to make the necessary changes.

Exercise: Self-Esteem Inventory. In my classes I always ask parents to list at least three things they feel good about as a parent. Inevitably people's faces go into contortions, and they feel awkward about trying to come up with three things. I gently tease them about how we are conditioned to look at our deficiencies and inadequacies, but in order to impart self-esteem to our kids, we have to start to focus on *our* strengths as well.

Take this opportunity to focus on what you are currently doing as a parent that's working! Yes, there are at least three things.

My strengths as a parent are⎯⎯⎯⎯⎯⎯⎯⎯⎯⎯⎯

⎯⎯⎯⎯⎯⎯⎯⎯⎯⎯⎯⎯⎯⎯⎯⎯⎯⎯⎯⎯⎯⎯

What gives you the greatest joy and brings you the most happiness as a parent?⎯⎯⎯⎯⎯⎯⎯⎯⎯⎯⎯⎯⎯

⎯⎯⎯⎯⎯⎯⎯⎯⎯⎯⎯⎯⎯⎯⎯⎯⎯⎯⎯⎯⎯⎯

Please feel free to share your insights with your kids!

Now, let's take a break for a moment. You bought this book because you want to be the best parent you can be. But not all of the process of parenting has to do with caring for and nurturing your children. Good parenting also require that you care for and nurture yourself. So, now, let's talk about you.

Chapter 2
PARENTS HAVE NEEDS, TOO!

"If you are not for yourself,
Who will be?
If you are only for you,
What's the purpose?
If not now, when?"
—Rabbi Hillel

Does your life feel chaotic and out of control? Do you continually feel overwhelmed and overextended? Is there too much to do and never enough time to do it? Do you feel like the low person on the totem pole when it comes to getting your needs met? If you answered yes to these questions, you, too, can join the millions of parents who are planning to run away from home by signing up for the first civilian flight to the moon!

All kidding aside, this chapter is for you. Stop and think for a minute about what happens if the CEO of a major multinational corporation is stressed out, or a pilot of a jetliner is feeling exhausted and mean-spirited, or the football team's quarterback is having a rotten day. In each case, all hell breaks loose and the game—be it making a profit, landing safely, or just plain winning—grinds to a halt. The same thing holds true for you in relation to your family. You're the center, the cornerstone upon which your entire family depends. When you let yourself be driven by perfectionism, guilt, and unattainably high standards, you become irritable, ornery, and unable to function well. Ignore your own needs long enough, and I guarantee, sooner or later Godzilla will emerge wreaking havoc and suffering on you and your entire family.

Being a parent is a tug-of-war between who we *think* we should be and who we are; between what we want to do and what we are actually able to do. Most of us have idealized images of what good parents should be, and are haunted by these images of perfection. Rather than confront the discrepancy between the idealized parent and our actual self, many of us feel inadequate and guilt-ridden because we can't match up to our own impossibly high standards.

THE MYTH OF PARENTAL SAINTHOOD

Many of us grew up watching *The Donna Reed Show, Leave It to Beaver,* and *Father Knows Best.* These nonexistent T.V. families were role models for how family life was supposed to be. Even now, the myth that parents are wise, godlike figures continues with the current favorite American prime-time family, the Huxtables of *The Cosby Show.*

Most of these television mothers had model-like figures and looked better cleaning their houses than most of us did at our weddings. None of these T.V. parents ever really lost their tempers, scrubbed toilets, worried about how to live within a budget, or screamed at their kids. No problem seemed too traumatic or complex for them to cure with a glass of milk and some cookies, or in Cliff Huxtable's case, some flawlessly droll remark. They exuded the saintly virtue of patience.

But how wise would Cliff Huxtable have been if his son were arrested for drugs? What would June Cleaver have said if Beaver were diagnosed with attention-deficit disorder? How would Donna Reed have broken the news of her divorce?

We all know that these prime-time moms and dads were too

good to be true, but in the far reaches of our minds many of us still aspire to be like them. We all have models of parental perfection stashed away in our psyches, models that we secretly believe we should be living up to.

THE SUPERPARENT SYNDROME

"I always feel like I'm failing at something," my client Sharon moaned sadly one day. "I'm supposed to have a perfect house, model children, cook gourmet balanced meals, volunteer as room mother and den mother, make costumes for my children's school plays, recycle my paper, glass, and tin and make compost for my organic garden, make sure my children have after-school enrichment activities, attend cultural events and keep up with current affairs, spend quality time with my children, and spend an hour a day exercising and at least two hours an evening with my husband having a meaningful conversation! All this while I hold down a full-time job and do it all with a smile. The fact is, I'm not doing any of it with a smile. I'm a nervous wreck. I snap at my husband and scream at my kids. I'm on a treadmill, and there's no way to get off!"

In the past the "average" family meant a breadwinning father and a mother who stayed home with the children. Today, only 4 percent of families fit this description.[1] In the majority of homes in America both parents now work outside the home. The typical child of preschool and elementary school age now lives with two parents who work full time. Blended families and single-parent families are fast becoming the rule rather than the exception. Our roles have changed along with the demands made on us, yet our internal standards for ourselves often are not a practical match for our actual living situations.

Sharon is driving herself crazy because she can't do it all. The truth is, none of us have it all or *do* it all. Something has to give, and we need to make compromises. And until we examine our beliefs and underlying motivations, we are driven by unrealistic standards that are impossible to attain.

"BUT MY MOM ALWAYS DID IT THIS WAY!"

Virginia Satir used to tell an interesting story about a Christmas roast. The recipe for baking the roast had been handed down from generation to generation. The recipe included the instructions "Always cut the roast in half before baking." One day the daughter in the family, who was married and had her own family, was in the kitchen preparing the Christmas roast. Suddenly a thought hit her. She turned to her own mother and asked, "Mom, why do you always cut the roast in half before baking it?" "I don't know," replied the mother. "I'm just following the recipe—ask Grandma." The granddaughter dutifully went to ask her grandmother, who replied without a moment's thought. "Oh," she said, "we always cut the roast in half because it was too big for the pot."[2]

Our own "shoulds" are often just as nonsensical. Once we examine them, we are often surprised to find that our most cherished "must do's" have no more practical place in our lives than cutting the Christmas roast had in the recipe.

LEARNING TO RESPECT OUR LIMITS

For many years one of my big "shoulds" was "A good parent should say yes to her child's desires whenever possible." The only problem was, a lot of times I really didn't want to. Time and time again I would end up saying yes to my daughter's requests when my feelings told me to do something entirely different. I was amazed that I had no trouble being clear about my feelings on this issue in the abstract. For example, I know without a doubt that parents shouldn't sacrifice their lives for their children's; parents need to have a life of their own both for their own good and for the good of their children; and parents shouldn't try to be and do everything for their kids. Despite the fact that I understood this on a conceptual level, when I was faced with the everyday reality of raising my daughter, I was in a state of utter confusion.

I instantly became a victim of the "nice guy" syndrome. I had it wired that saying "yes" meant "I love you" and saying "no" meant "I don't love you." When we suffer from this kind of crazy thinking, we act dishonestly and filter our responses through our own confusion and guilt. And then comes trouble.

I was in the middle of my aerobics exercise tape one afternoon when my daughter and her two friends came in and pleaded with me to take them to the park. I thought about it for a moment and my internal dialogue went something like this: "I really don't feel like cutting my workout short, but it would be nice for the girls to get out and do something fun. Good mothers go out of their way for their kids. I should go." This happened within a matter of seconds. Before I had time to reconsider I was on automatic pilot and dutifully off my mat, out the door, and on my way to the park.

When we arrived, the girls immediately began to climb on the monkey bars and slide down the new circular slide. Within a matter of minutes my daughter came running over to me whining, "I want to go home. Carolyn and Heather are hogging all the good stuff." I practically spat through a clenched jaw, "You wanted to come here! Now play on something else until they give you a turn." "No, I only want to play on the new twister slide. I don't want to do anything else." She began to cry while I walked with her over to her friends and played referee. They played for another few minutes, but the fighting persisted until, utterly exasperated, I decided to take them home. By the time we got home I was angry and resentful that what started out to be a mission of mercy had turned into such a hassle. I started out to be such a nice guy and ended up acting like the Wicked Witch of the West. How did this happen?

First of all, I really didn't feel like interrupting my workout to go to the park. I thought I was being nice and generous, and yet when I reviewed the situation I realized that the last thing I really wanted to do was to go out with the kids. I had really wanted some time to myself. Why was it so hard for me to say a simple no? I saw how confused I could become about my true feelings in relationship to my child.

Numerous books and articles have been written in the last ten years on how to foster peak performance in corporations. Study after study details the specific conditions that are required to produce optimal results in corporate employees: open communication, clearly defined expectations, supportive working conditions, regularly scheduled breaks, a sense of teamwork, consideration for personal needs and concerns. Doing good work as a parent is just like performing well in any other arena of challenging work. And yet most of us tend to act as though none of these principles applies when it comes to our most important, challenging, and demanding job. Time and time again we expect ourselves to be peak performers under conditions that are far less than optimal.

We wouldn't dream of driving our car when the gas gauge reads empty or the oil light is flashing. We wouldn't think of asking our child to pull an all-nighter to prepare for final exams, yet we are continually pushing ourselves past the breaking point and ignoring the fact that there will inevitably be negative repercussions.

THE GUILT TRAP

We demand that we act more generously than we feel, give more than we have to give, and push ourselves beyond our limits. This is a surefire recipe for disaster. How long do you think you can function under these conditions? Not very long and certainly not very well.

Petra, a mother in one of my seminars, came into the class and reported, "I can't believe how easy it is to fall back into the role of supermom. I thought, after last week's discussion, that I had buried my superwoman cape, but I found myself wearing it again without even thinking."

"What happened?" one of the parents inquired. Petra rolled

her eyes. "I had just come home from a very stressful day at work when my daughter Margaret met me at the door and immediately began complaining that she had nothing to wear to her best friend's birthday party. I had planned on coming home and relaxing, but she begged me to wash and iron her favorite outfit. Before I could stop myself, I said, 'Sure, honey, bring me your clothes.' I rummaged through the pantry for the laundry detergent, but we were out. 'I'll be right back,' I said in my semi-cheerful voice and headed out the door with the intention of driving to the supermarket.

"As soon as I got into the car and started the engine it hit me! Here I was, making myself into a pretzel one more time, trying to be the all-nurturing earth mother to my kids. As I allowed myself my feelings, I realized that I was angry and frustrated for so easily falling into the superwoman trap without even noticing it.

"I decided to tell Margaret the truth instead of suffering in silence. I marched back into the house and said, 'I'm really too tired to make an emergency run to the store.' Margaret was upset for a second and then she became solution oriented.

" 'How about if you just iron one of my wrinkled dresses?' she suggested. 'That won't be so hard, Mommy.' I thought about it for a moment and that sounded workable. Margaret climbed up on the counter, got down the iron, and filled it with water. We ended up by turning a fiasco into a family project. Nevertheless, I hope I learned my lesson. I can't believe how easy it is to say *yes* when I mean *no*."

When we are honest with our children about our feelings, limits, and needs, we give them the chance to consider another person besides themselves.

NO IS NOT A FOUR-LETTER WORD

If you have trouble saying no, you are in good company. Harvard psychologist Carol Gilligan reports that a woman's concern for others is central to the way she makes decisions. Men often make decisions based on principles. Women, much more concerned with the impact the decision will have on the people involved, consequently are loath to say no.[3]

Frequently we feel that when we say no we are not rejecting a request, but we are rejecting the other person. And since we certainly don't want to reject our children, we resist saying no. Furthermore, if we see "no" as a rejection, chances are we ourselves hate to be told no. Consequently, we also hesitate in saying no because we don't want anyone to say no to us (not that this ever works). To most people, unless they've learned otherwise, "no" conjures up thoughts of selfishness, weakness, anger, rejection, failure, and stubbornness, to name but a few. It's not surprising some of us have trouble with this little word.

Another obstacle to saying no is our fear of arousing anger in someone else. For many of us anger is uncomfortable and to be avoided at all cost.

However, if we deny our own needs and do whatever others ask of us, all we are likely to do is win the martyr-of-the year award. And along with the award comes a sense of powerlessness, resentment, rage, and decreased self-esteem. Not exactly emotional conditions that any of us want to go out of our way to cultivate.

Remember, you have every right to say "no" to something you don't wish to do. When you say "yes" but you really want to say "no," you are being dishonest; worse yet, those close to you—especially your children—will sense your dishonesty even if they can't consciously put their finger on the discrepancy they are sensing. The final result is that they will have a hard time trusting you. When kids can count on you to say "no" when you mean "no," there is a great sense of relief. They know you will say what you mean, and they don't have to try to second-guess you. You do others a disservice when you don't express your true thoughts and feelings.

The truth is, learning to say "no" is an acquired skill. And, like learning how to swim, you get better with practice. Using this powerful two-letter word doesn't mean you will never do a favor for a friend again or accept another invitation about which you're somewhat ambivalent. However, when you make a decision to go against your feelings, it will be your adult decision, not the decision of your guilt demons. Moreover, learning to say "no" can dramatically increase your time and help you to feel better about yourself and less resentful of others.

In many cases learning to say no simply requires that you take the time to consider what you really want to do. Rather than reacting with a "yes," you can say, "Let me get back to you about that." Very few things require an immediate decision. Then ask yourself, "Do I really want to do this? Is it important to me? What will I gain by saying yes? What's the worst thing that will happen if I say no? Is this genuinely good for me? Or am I being seduced by the 'I can do it all' syndrome?"

Virginia Satir, a pioneer in the field of family therapy and self-esteem, introduced me to something called a Yes-and-No medallion. The medallion is a coin with "Yes" written in large letters, and below it, "Thank you for noticing me and asking me. The answer is Yes." On the other side, in equally beautiful letters, it says "No," and below it, "Thank you for noticing and asking me, but it doesn't fit for me right now, and may never. The answer is no." She suggested that before responding to a request, you pick up your coin and really ask yourself, "Does this fit for me now, or am I better off saying thank you for asking, but the answer is no?" Or is the real answer, "Yes, thank you for noticing me and asking me. What you ask serves me well right now"? Satir would always emphasize that in neither case does it mean "I love you" or "I don't love you."

I found this idea very helpful, since I, too, was a trained people-pleaser and found that my automatic response to any request was yes.

In my case I didn't use a coin. Instead, I decided to go down to the beach and find a special beach stone. I wrote YES in big letters on one side, and NO on the other. I keep my Yes-and-No rock on my desk and look at it whenever I am asked to make a decision. It acts as a reminder to take a moment to consider what is really best for me before I jump in with an answer.

FOR EVERYONE'S SAKE, TAKE CARE OF YOURSELF

Melanie came into my seminar one evening looking exhausted and defeated. One of the other participants asked her if she was feeling all right. Close to tears, she shook her head and started to recount her day. "This morning Alan and I got up as usual. But Alan now has a job that's forty-five minutes from home, so he dashes out of the house before breakfast, and I'm left with the brunt of the morning routine. I went in and woke up Leslie, my four-year-old, and then rousted out David, the nine-year-old, and sent him into the bathroom to shower. Leslie insists that I crawl back in bed with her for fifteen minutes to cuddle, which I did begrudgingly. When I could finally tear myself away from her, I got up, laid out her clothes, then hurried into the kitchen to put out an assortment of breakfast cereals for the kids. While they were eating breakfast, I raced around the house getting their books and things ready for school and fixing school lunches.

"Once I finished getting Leslie dressed, we made a mad dash for the car, and off to school they went. By the end of the morning routine I felt frazzled, and I'm not really sure why. Nothing terrible happened, but I felt more like a robot with run-down batteries than a mother."

"What about you?" several parents asked.

"What?" Melanie looked startled, as if she didn't comprehend the sense of the question.

"What did *you* have for breakfast? And how about your shower? Did you leave that part out?" asked the class.

"No way!" Melanie responded as she stared at them with a dazed expression on her face. "There's just no time for me."

"It seems that everyone else's needs and wants come before yours," pressed the class members, "and that there is no place for you other than to be the nurturer and caretaker."

"Yes, that's exactly how I feel," Melanie blurted out sadly. "I feel like there's not enough time for me, that I come last or not at all!"

"How do you feel about that?" I gently probed. "I hate it," she said. "I get really angry and yell at my kids for no apparent reason, and David cowers and wonders why I'm always so edgy. I can't go on like this!" And she broke down in tears. I told Melanie that her reaching her limit was good news. Although the realization was painful to her at the moment, she now had the opportunity to do something that would bring her and her needs back into the picture.

With coaching from other participants and myself, Melanie began to get up a half hour earlier and go for a walk around the neighborhood with a friend. When she came back, she would wake up the kids and jump in the shower instead of going back to bed with Leslie. Over the next several weeks she stopped racing around the house gathering up her children's belongings, and began to sit down with the kids and have breakfast with them, directing them to gather their own books, etc.

When she returned to class for the next session, the other class members were anxious to hear about her progress. "I can't believe how hard it is to take time for myself," Melanie admitted. "Even though I know how essential it is, it's still so easy to slip back into trying to do it all. I can see I need to regularly recommit myself to my own care."

Why is it so difficult for us to take care of ourselves? Melanie was raised in a family where her mother subscribed to the suffer-and-sacrifice style of parenting. She also was the oldest of three children, and her family role was to be a caretaker—the Responsible One. So she believed that Doing It All was expected of her. She also discovered that she had bought the idea that good mothers put their children's needs first or they don't really care. She thought that it was blasphemy to consider her own feelings, needs, and limitations. With the support of the class she was able to loosen these restrictive beliefs, and her compulsion to make counterproductive sacrifices began to change.

The needs of our children deserve our attention and consideration, especially when they are infants and least able to take care of themselves. But as they grow, we must gradually bring our own needs back into the picture. We can begin to move from so-called ideal parents who make a multitude of sacrifices for their kids, to what pediatrician Donald Winnicott called "good enough parents."[4] We have to give up the idea of being perfect parents as well as recognize that there are no perfect children. Perfection is out of reach of mortal human beings, but being "good enough" is well within our grasp. "Good enough" parents can raise healthy children and stay healthy themselves. "Perfect" parents are either failing all the time, or are lying all the time—both to themselves and their kids. The word "perfection" linked with parenthood is a guaranteed recipe for disaster.

WHAT DO YOU REALLY WANT FOR YOURSELF?

In my seminars I ask parents to do a self-care inventory. I reassure them that this inventory is only for them—that no one else needs to see it, so there's no one to impress.

Take a moment and answer the following questions:

1. What do you do for fun?
2. When was the last time you took time to be with a friend, had a massage, or did something purely nurturing for yourself?

3. Do you exercise regularly?

4. What do you do to unwind and relax?

5. How do you feel about your body? Do you like the way you look?

6. Are you within ten pounds of your ideal weight? What do you do to maintain or improve your appearance?

7. What is your overall attitude toward life? Do you lean toward optimism or pessimism?

8. When you are faced with challenges, is your reaction generally more positive or negative? Are you content and happy most of the time?

9. How often do you feel irritable because you are over-stressed and exhausted?

10. How frequently are you sick?

11. Do you ask for help when you need it?

12. Do you have as much physical contact and nurturing as you would like?

13. Do you express a wide range of emotions?

14. How often do you say yes when you want to say no?

15. Are you doing what you want to be doing with your life?

16. Whom do you talk to when you're upset?

17. Do you look forward to coming home at the end of the day?

Once parents have had a chance to answer the above questions, I ask them to evaluate how well they think they are doing with their own self care, on a scale of one to ten, one being absolutely abominable and neglectful of oneself and ten being terrifically self-caring and nurturing.

Circle the number below that most honestly represents where you currently are with your self-care.

Utter neglect 1 2 3 4 5 6 7 8 9 10 Well cared for

Please be honest with yourself. Remember, this is just between you and you.

Make a list of what you are currently doing for yourself that you feel good about._____

_____

_____

What are ten things you love to do?_____

_____

_____

When was the last time you did any of them?_____

_____

What areas of your own self-care need some attention?

_____

_____

_____

What are you going to do to improve on the neglected areas? Be specific._____

_____

_____

You are your children's best role model. Children learn by example. One of the greatest gifts you can give your kids is the model of a fulfilled, vital person.[5]

SCHEDULE TIME

Many people feel that time for themselves is stolen time in which they are playing hooky from more important endeavors! Actually scheduling self-nurturing activities is a way to trick our guilt demons. When we schedule personal time for ourselves, we make it legitimate.

When scheduling time, keep it simple. The fewer details, the better. One way to guard against the tyranny of the "shoulds" overriding your plans is to make plans with a friend.

By using the buddy system, you are less likely to cancel your date.

Let your family know in advance that you are planning to take some time for yourself and that this time is special time just for you.

HONORING YOURSELF: YOUR OWN SELF-ESTEEM

We are the initiators and models of our children's self-esteem, and while we can't teach what we don't know, there is good news: If, like so many of us, you have arrived at parenting with feelings of low self-worth, take heart—there are innumerable opportunities to counteract your past by making changes in the present. All we have to do is to keep our eyes open. I guarantee that as you wrestle with the issues of your child's self-esteem, you will also find yourself confronting self-worth issues of your own. For example, we have no trouble seeing that it is important to encourage our children to believe in themselves, and yet it is surprisingly difficult for many of us to give our own adult selves that same encouragement. It sounds illogical when you say it, but most of us secretly consider taking care of ourselves to be an impermissible indulgence. Moreover, the thought that *to take care of yourself* is an essential part of taking care of your family might sound acceptable in the abstract, but putting it into actual practice is quite a different affair. Below are several suggestions that can enhance your self-esteem:

SELF-ESTEEM BUILDERS

1. Celebrate your strengths. It is essential that you recognize your own strengths and positive qualities. Take a moment and reflect on your strengths and abilities. List at least five._____

_____

_____

In my seminars I ask participants to complete the statement, "I like myself because" in writing on 3″×5″ index cards. I recommend to them that they read their statements either to themselves or with a friend at least once a day as a reminder of their positive qualities.

Focusing on your strengths especially at the times when you are getting down on yourself requires that you develop a system of positive support by using daily reminders. When I first started to shift my attention to my positive qualities, I used a system of reminder notes around my house. I posted little signs with positive phrases, such as "I love and accept you just the way you are" on my bathroom mirror, "I am a nurturing, caring, committed parent" next to my bed, and "Life is meant to be fun, and I am fully enjoying it" on the refrigerator. Put these reminder notes where you can easily and naturally see them.

I know these techniques may sound silly, and you may feel awkward at first, but do them anyway. Most parents resist using the notes or the 3″×5″ cards until I nag them unmercifully for a week or two. But once they get past their initial self-consciousness, they are, almost without exception, astonished and delighted with the effectiveness of these tools. They come back to class with glowing stories of how the reminders helped them. Give it a try. Dare to be different!

2. *Cultivate an attitude of acceptance and self-respect.* If you are critical and hard on yourself, you tend to be critical of others. On the other hand, if you are compassionate and accepting of yourself, you will be more accepting of others. This is easy advice to give, but how do you implement it?

I was sitting on my bed one day, and I got an image of my inner critic. I decided to give her a name, since she was such a regular visitor in my life. I thought for a moment, and a name popped into my head. She was definitely a Bertha. There were times in the past when Bertha would get so loud that I felt completely defeated, miserable, and like a worm. At these times I would sit down and have a talk with her and tell her to shut up and leave me alone. In effect, I would defend myself against my inner critic. At one point it got so bad that I decided to send her on a long cruise to the Bahamas. That worked pretty well, but periodically she reappears and I have to put her back in her place.

Would you want a friend who was constantly critical of you, blamed you for everything that went wrong, put you down no matter what you did, kept a running tally of all your failures, and beat you up for even the smallest mistakes? Not if she were the last person alive. Yet repeatedly we give in to this tyrant. It's time to take a moment and close your eyes and give your inner critic a name. Get to know him or her more directly, then take an 8½″ × 11″ sheet of paper and fold it down the center. Make two columns, one for your critical voice and one for your defending self. Then, without censoring, write the critical statements you frequently make about yourself.

CRITIC: "You're stupid."

DEFENDER: "No I'm not."

CRITIC: "I can't believe you told your sister her son could stay with you for a week while she and her husband went on vacation."

DEFENDER: "I wanted to help her out! It's my choice anyway—now, get off my case."

CRITIC: "Don't you have any smarts? You're a real sucker. No wonder people take advantage of you."

DEFENDER: "If you'd stop harping at me, maybe I could say no more easily."

CRITIC: "You have 'kick me' written all over you. Smarten up."

DEFENDER: "Be quiet and stop talking to me like that. If you have something to say, you'll have to say it in a nicer way or I don't want to hear it."

When you notice that you feel discouraged, depressed, and as if you just don't like yourself, your critic has you in her grips. Take charge, bring in your protective nurturing voice. It's impossible to feel good about yourself when there is a voice in your head continually telling you what you're doing wrong or how bad you are.

3. Recognize and appreciate your achievements, and express satisfaction in your accomplishments. Most of us were raised to give others compliments, not ourselves. Well, it's time to stop eating humble pie. In my seminars I ask all participants to choose a partner, and for ninety seconds to brag nonstop about the good in themselves. At first a rush of fear runs through the room. But once people start the process, they inevitably finish the exercise feeling exhilarated, with an increased sense of healthy pride in themselves.

We must also become more comfortable with receiving compliments. I love to cook and take pride in it, yet I would always deflect the praise of my dinner guests, saying, "Oh, it was nothing. You should come over when I really have time to cook." I deflected their compliments. Let yourself enjoy the friendly praise of others.

Giving ourselves messages of appreciation and self-validation teaches our kids to do the same. "I love the way the flower garden turned out." "It feels good to have finished wallpapering the bathroom." "I like the way this outfit looks on me." It's simply telling the truth! This isn't vanity!

4. Value and express your thoughts and opinions. I have a friend who rarely expresses a strong opinion about anything. When I ask her where she wants to go for dinner, her standard response is, "I don't care." If I say, "How about Italian?," she'll say fine. Then if I suggest Greek, she says, "Greek's good, too." "What about Thai food? Do you want to go for Thai food?" "Yeah that's fine." Inevitably I decide where we end up going, and feel frustrated with her passivity.

My friend's lack of personal expression translates into every part of her life. She has trouble saying no to people, and frequently finds herself overextended and stressed out. She has difficulty standing up for *her* needs in her marriage, and she is often withdrawn and painfully shy in social settings. Of course, by playing it safe, she fits in everywhere, but doesn't really ever have herself anywhere she goes.

People with high self-esteem aren't afraid to express their opinions, even if they are different from others'. I'm not advocating arrogance and bullying. I'm saying that being willing to stand up for what you believe in and making your thoughts and feelings known is another way of offering yourself a vote of self-confidence, of saying, "I matter."

5. *Get in the habit of giving yourself a message of love and appreciation for the unique being you are.*
What qualities make you special and unique? List at least five!

Now, take a moment and appreciate the precious miracle that you are, the tremendous possibilities that you have.

And for another moment imagine what your life would be like if you woke up every morning with a message of love and appreciation in your thoughts. A message that sounded something like, "I love me, I value me." What would happen if you got into the habit of saying this to yourself several times a day? Wouldn't the world look like a better place?

Remember, the degree to which you love and value yourself is the degree to which you can love and value others. Conversely the degree to which you devalue yourself, you, of necessity, devalue others. And of course when you devalue yourself, you want to force others to make up for your feelings of deficiency.

Our real resources are not our money or our material possessions, but our ability to see, to hear, to taste, to touch, to feel, to think, to move, to speak, and to use our ability to choose. These are our true riches.

YOU DESERVE A BREAK TODAY

Let's look at some more techniques for improving your sense of value and self-respect that can be used as antidotes to the toxic messages from your inner critic.

Mirror Exercise: All too often, it's looking in the mirror that initiates the critical inner dialogue: "Oh, no! Do I have another gray hair?" "Look at those bags under my eyes." "Am I going bald?" "Is that a zit on my face?" "I don't believe it! Even my earlobes have wrinkles!" We all do it. However, now, I am going to suggest that you do something entirely different. Either sit or stand in front of a mirror. Look yourself in the eyes and focus on loving yourself. Then, speaking out loud, begin to appreciate yourself for everything you feel good about. Mention all your special qualities and accomplishments. For example: "I love you. You're such a good friend. I really appreciate the way you got the kids to bed on time tonight without yelling. Good work. I like your sense of humor. I really appreciate the way you are keeping your word and exercising at least three times a week." Talk with yourself the way a nurturing friend or parent would.

Restrict your comments to positive, supportive, nurturing statements. By the way, it's a good idea to alert your family to what you are doing, so they don't think you've lost it and call the men in white.

The first day I went into my nurturing monologue, my daughter came racing into the bathroom. "Mom, who were you talking to?" When I told her what I was doing, she walked away shaking her head and saying, "Oh, no. I pray none of my friends ever hear you. You've really lost it this time. Do you *have to* do this? You're too weird!" I laughed and went back to talking to myself.

It will undoubtedly feel awkward when you begin, but stay

with it and it will become easier. Spend about five minutes giving yourself this loving attention. You deserve it.

Try doing the exercise every morning and evening for a month. It takes about twenty-one days to establish a new habit. Notice the positive effect this has on your self-esteem and overall attitude.

Exercise: Practice Being. Spend ten minutes a day doing nothing in a quiet place. You can sit in the sun, lie on your bed, sit in a bath. Choose how you want to spend your ten minutes. The point of this exercise is simple. We spend so much of our lives *doing*, and we need time each day for just *being*. Focus on your breathing as you relax and enjoy being with yourself.

The famous scholar and mythologist Joseph Campbell often talked about the value of having what he called a "sacred place":

> This is an absolute necessity for anybody today. You must have a room, or a certain hour or so a day, where you don't know what was in the newspapers that morning, you don't know who your friends are, you don't know what you owe anybody, you don't know what anybody owes to you. This is a place where you can simply experience and bring forth what you are and what might be. This is a place of creative incubation. At first you may find nothing happens there. But if you have a sacred place and use it, something eventually will happen. . . .
>
> Our life has become so economic and practical in its orientation that, as you get older, the claims of the moment upon you are so great, you hardly know where the hell you are, or what it is you intended. You are always doing something that is required of you. Where is your bliss station? You have to try to find it. Get a phonograph and put on the music that you really love, even if it's corny music that nobody else respects. Or get the book you like to read. In your sacred place you get the "thou" feeling of life. . . .[6]

Now, let's talk more about the kids.

Chapter 3
FALLING IN LOVE WITH YOUR KIDS

"Children who are truly loved unconsciously know themselves to be valued. This knowledge is worth more than gold. . . . The feeling of being valuable—'I am a valuable person'—is essential to mental health and is a cornerstone of self-discipline. It is a direct product of parental love."
—M. Scott Peck, *The Road Less Traveled*[1]

When I ask parents in my seminars, "How many of you love your kids?," they look at me as though I'm crazy. Of course we love our children! Then I ask, "How many of you knew you were loved by your parents while you were growing up?" Most people raise their hands. Finally I ask, "How many of you felt loved?" Fewer people raise their hands. Sometimes parents who really love their kids don't know how to convey it. The real question isn't whether you love your kids or not, but how well you are able to demonstrate your love and caring so that your children really feel loved.

Conveying our love to our children is priority number one. It needs to come before any other aspect of the parenting process. Kids don't care how much you know until they know how much you care. Before you offer correction, guidance, or suggestions, your unconditional love needs to be the basis of your relationship with your children.

Remember when you fell in love with someone? Can you

recall how you felt? When you love someone, you can't wait to see him. You spend hours talking, getting to know one another. You're interested in every word he says. You want to know everything about him. You're fascinated with his history, his interests, aspirations, and dreams. You treat him as if he is the most important person in the world. You touch him often and are childlike and playful together. You do special loving things for one another—send cards, flowers, get tickets to the football game, or cook him a surprise dinner. When you are together, the rest of the world seems to fade away. You genuinely enjoy each other, celebrate his being, and thank God for his presence in your life.

To build your children's self-esteem, you have to fall in love with them. How do you do that? Well, you fall in love with them just as you would with anyone else.

Here are nine basic ingredients for falling in love with your kids.

1. Spend time together.
2. Develop common interests.
3. Play together.
4. Talk together.
5. Touch each other.
6. Tell your children often that you love them.
7. Treat your kids as if they are the most important people in the world.
8. Create lasting memories.
9. Celebrate their uniqueness.

Let's explore those ingredients in detail.

1. SPEND TIME TOGETHER

Could you fall in love with someone if you spent an hour a day together, and during that time you were fixing dinner, folding the laundry, or reading the newspaper? Of course not. But we are busy people, and often that's all the time we feel we have to spare for our kids.

Studies show that parents in the United States spend less time with their children than in almost any other country of the world, including Russia.

A research team at the University of Michigan Institute of Social Research did a national random sample of six-hundred adults over the span of a year. The families who were interviewed varied in lifestyles from rural to urban dwellers. What the researchers found was that working mothers spend an average of eleven minutes daily of quality time (defined as exclusive play or teaching time) with their children during the weekdays, and about thirty minutes per day on the weekends. Fathers spend about eight minutes of quality time with their kids on weekdays, and fourteen minutes on weekends. Think it's better if you don't work outside the home? Surprise! Nonworking mothers spend an average of thirteen minutes of quality time per day with their children. Pretty startling![2]

These statistics exist not because we don't care about our kids, but because we assume that the time we spend with them while also taking care of the necessities of life should suffice. However, the plain truth is, nothing takes the place of spending focused time with your child.

When we set aside special time for our children, they in turn say to themselves, "I must be important to my mom or dad for her/him to take this time to be just with me." This kind of special time isn't just something nice to do, it is critical in building your child's sense of self-esteem.

By the way, I'm not for a minute suggesting that it's easy to set aside special time. With our demanding schedules it sometimes seems impossible to fulfill all of our commitments. I continually hear the cry, "There's so much to do, and not enough hours in the day."

And don't worry, I'm not recommending that you give up your career to devote all of your time and energy to your kids, or that you subscribe to the martyr school of parenting, where your kids' needs always come before your own. The key is to balance our own valid needs with those of our children. This may require a reordering of priorities.

It is far too easy to lose sight of the wonder of our children amid the daily routines of running a household and/or often holding a job; we forget the preciousness of the present moment.

There are numerous ways of spending effective time with your children.

Take Your Kids to a Special Place

Take them somewhere out of the ordinary, so that they will have a memory of sharing a special place with you.

When my daughter was eight, I took her to a sacred Anasazi Indian site outside of Santa Fe, New Mexico, where we were living. It was something I'd always meant to do with her, but somehow I had not ever managed to allocate the time. Even on this day I felt guilty because of all the other "important" things I should have been doing instead. Nevertheless, we went.

The site was in the desert, and had Indian petroglyphs and pottery shards on it. We carried paper, ink, and an old tennis ball wrapped in a sock to make stone rubbings.

As it turned out, we spent the whole day sitting on the cliffs overlooking a vast expanse of desert making stone rubbings, picnicking, collecting pottery shards, and sunning ourselves on the rocks like lizards.

On the drive back Ama unrolled her pictures and looked at them proudly. She was obviously delighted that I had shared this special place with her. As soon as we arrived home, she took her rubbings and her bag of shards and ran over to her friend Alba's house to show off her treasures. That evening as I said good night to her, Ama smiled up at me and asked, "Can we take Alba and Celia to show them our special Indian place?" I wondered to myself how I could have ever doubted the worth of this day.

When you share a special place with your kids, you include them in your world in a unique way. You say to them, "I enjoy you and want to share a special part of me with you." As a result they feel valued and respected.

Make a Date

A mother came up to me after one of my lectures and said she had read every book she could find on sibling rivalry and had tried various techniques, but nothing seemed to work. "I have a six-year-old son, and a daughter who's one and a half, and Bobby seems to be angry and jealous of the baby no matter what I do!" she lamented. After she listed all the techniques she had tried, I suggested that she make a regular date with her son to spend time with him alone. I explained to her that when you have several children, the need for one-to-one time is even greater. By making a date for focused time, you give your child a break from the constant competition for your attention, plus you promote greater cooperation between your kids.

One of the toughest things your child has to learn is to share you. By making a "date," your children will know that they can count on being with you on a regular basis. It adds to their sense of security and satisfies their need to feel special.

"The Spotlight's on Me!"

Children thrive on being the center of attention. We give our kids the spotlight when it's their birthday, bar mitzvah, confirmation, or special occasion. However, it's wonderful to do this more regularly.

There is an activity I teach in my seminars called "Star for the Evening." On a specific night one child gets to be the star. The star receives the family's undivided attention either during dinner or after dinner at a show-and-tell hour. The special child has an opportunity to talk about any accomplishments, special activities, or whatever is really interesting to him or her. After the child has presented his chosen subject, he receives a standing ovation. This means that he stands in front of you and everyone applauds, cheers, and hoots as a way of celebrating him—not necessarily because he did anything outstanding, but simply because he exists.

One father reported that in his family their son brought home all the merit badges he had been working on at Cub Scouts. He showed them to his family and described what he had to do to earn each one. "My son just basked in the spotlight. He couldn't believe that we were all paying attention to him, even his two sisters." "Tomorrow night it's my turn," the dad said, only half joking. We all enjoy being center stage periodically.

When you spend special time with your child, you'll both experience a sense of closeness, satisfaction, and increased self-esteem. And special time can be throwing a Frisbee, getting a frozen yogurt, going for a walk, playing Candyland. It need not be complicated. Spending time with your kids is like putting money in the bank. As your "account balance" increases, you will gain interest in the years to come through raising emotionally healthy, secure children.

2. DEVELOP COMMON INTERESTS

One day when Ama was six, I sat down with her and said, "Tomorrow's Sunday—let's spend the day together. What would you like to do?" Rather than giving her specific choices, I intentionally left the question general, because I was curious to see what her interests were. She thought for a moment. "I want to plant a garden." I was surprised. I had no idea that she even liked gardening!

We went to the store and picked out some seeds. She chose sweet peas, radishes, lettuce, and snapdragons. Then we went out into the backyard, and I started to clear away the weeds and debris from the last year. But I quickly realized that we gardened quite differently.

Ama opened all the packages of seeds and was ready to plant them. She didn't want to bother preparing the ground. I gave up trying to be systematic, and we planted a row of peas. I made the row; she dropped in the seeds, patted down the earth, and watered them. That was the extent of her interest. Then she went over and lay down on the grass, and I joined her. We looked up at the clouds and imagined animals out of the cloud formations. We made up stories about the dragons, castles, and ballet dancers we saw. We had a great time together. I learned that she and I loved to make up stories and that we liked to dig in the dirt, two interests that we share to this day.

Identifying common interests can have unexpected side benefits: This summer, as I was out once again preparing the garden plot, Ama, who is now fifteen, came out and helped me pull weeds and pick rocks out of the plot. While we worked side by side, she began to talk about her relationship with her father and how sad she felt that she didn't see him more often. Our common love of gardening provided a bubble of intimacy that allowed us to talk about more sensitive subjects than might have been possible at other times.

Gardening has become a way for us to connect through an activity that we both enjoy. By sharing the experience over the years, we have created a safe space to talk about difficult issues that are so easily neglected in the rush of our busy lives.

3. PLAY TOGETHER

"Why do the elephants paint their toes red?"
"I don't know. Why?"
"So they can hide in cherry trees."

"I never saw an elephant in a cherry tree."
"See, it works!"

One of the essential ingredients for falling in love with your children is to have fun together. "Will you play with me?" is something you hear over and over from children. Having fun comes naturally to children, but most of us have to rekindle our playful inner child.

In my seminars I have parents do an exercise in which, by answering a series of questions, they begin to remember what they were like when they were the age of one of their children. The questions I ask are simple. Try to answer them yourself:

What was your nickname as a kid?

What did you enjoy doing?

What was your favorite toy? Activity? Game?

Who was your best friend?

Then I ask, "When was the last time you did any of these things? And are you willing to do one of the things you enjoyed as a child with *your* children in the next couple of days?"[3]

This exercise helps parents get into the spirit of play. Many of us have received messages throughout our adult lives that we should earnestly buckle down to work. Responsibly we put away our playful parts to deal with the more "important" business of the world. But to paraphrase the old adage, "All work and no play makes us dull parents."

Children appreciate it immensely when we lighten up and become playful. This play can take many forms, from rough-housing, to playing catch, to acting silly by talking in a funny accent, to jumping in a pile of freshly raked leaves, finger painting, playing hide-and-seek, etc. Use your imagination!

I'll never forget the time that I spontaneously asked Ama to go roller-skating with me. We drove down to the park, and I sat in the car putting on my old blue suede skates. As I laced them up, I began having second thoughts. "Maybe this wasn't such a good idea after all," I said to Ama. "I haven't skated in years."

"Oh, Mom, don't worry, I'll show you what to do," she reassured me. Hah! Merely getting up the ramp in the parking garage was a nearly insurmountable challenge. However, with a lot of help and perseverance (and general humiliation on my part), we made it to the street.

As I waited at the curb for the light to change, I realized that my real problem was stopping! I raced across the street as the light turned green, only to find the curb ahead of me. I jumped over it and started to fall, and just barely caught my balance. Ama gracefully skated over to me, and we both burst out laughing. "Way to go, Mom," she snickered. I was laughing so hard, I was convinced I would wet my pants.

In between giggles Ama showed me how to use the rubber stopper on the front of my skates to slow myself down and stop. We must have spent an hour racing up and down the paved path. Once I felt more confident, she taught me how to do some fancier footwork. It was a fabulous afternoon for both of us. In this experience we switched roles. Ama became the expert in skating and was able to teach me something new. I became her student and temporary playmate.

Play can be much simpler. One of my clients and her six-year-old son came up with a secret phrase that is totally silly: "I love you, Beeze Bamaloos!" They play a game of trying to sneak the phrase into their conversations unexpectedly, at which point both burst out laughing. The game makes no sense to anyone else, but it is a source of endless delight to both mother and son.

4. TALK TOGETHER

I wish I could record your conversations with your kids and let you listen to them. I think a lot of you would find that they aren't very interesting. The bulk of our interactions with our kids is made up of maintenance talk. Did you brush your teeth? Is your bed made? How did you do on your test? Did you finish your homework? You may ask, "What else do I find to talk to them about?"

The answer is simple: Something real. Tell them about your childhood, and what it was like for you. Do they know anything more about you except that you walked five miles to school in a driving snowstorm? Tell them about the street where you lived, how mad you used to get at your mom, how much you loved your best friend, and how you despised your algebra teacher. Children are fascinated to learn about their parents, especially stories where you were the same age they are now. I tell Ama about having every record that Martha and the Vandellas ever made, about belonging to the Fabian fan club, and about the time my best friend, Joan Barone, stole my boyfriend Tony. I tell her about how I used to get up an hour early every morning before school so I could tease my hair and get my "bubble" to look just right. Let your kids know you.

Talking about your past or your kids' past has special dividends, because children benefit immensely by having a sense of their roots and heritage.

They also love to hear stories about what *they* were like when they were babies, and what they did and said as they grew. (This is especially essential for kids who are adopted.)

There is a game I made up called "When You Were Little." It's a way of giving your child an oral history of the different stages he or she went through. What you do is simply recount different memories you have of the things they did at different ages. For example. "When you were a baby, you used to make such wonderful cooing sounds. They sounded French and Japanese: 'Hagone' and 'Irree.' When you were two, you would walk around carrying your favorite doll, Big Dolly, every where you went. When you were five, you used to like to help me make Jell-O and pick carrots from the garden. When you were six, you would only wear dresses. In first grade you read me a story from your first reader, called 'Go, Dog, Go.' "

Listening to these tales, they are not only able to see how they have grown and changed, they also feel important and reassured by our fascination with them and the incidents of their lives. When you give your kids the gift of these oral histories, you'll find that they will ask to hear the same stories over and over again. If you make a mistake or omit an important detail, they will supply you with the corrections or missing details that you left out on the twelfth retelling.

Opening Our Hearts to Our Kids

Another fertile topic of conversation parents often mistakenly stay away from is their own feelings. Tell your kids about how you feel when you hear Glenn Gould play Bach's *Goldberg Variations;* how you feel when you see an Ansel Adams photograph. Let them hear your good feelings as well as your stormy ones. When we share ourselves with our kids, it gives them permission to express themselves. Share your hopes, concerns, and dreams with your children. When your kids feel you are a vulnerable, feeling human being, then they can let some of their own real feelings show. They will feel closer to you.

Encouraging children to talk about their own fantasies and worries requires that we not only make space for uninterrupted time, but that we share information about ourselves as well.

On a recent visit to my parents' house I decided to rummage through their basement searching for memorabilia from my childhood. I started pulling boxes full of old sixties records and moldy school papers out of the closet. Then, in the midst of a pile of photographs, I found some poetry I had written in high school and college. There was one particular assignment that I remembered with great fondness. It was a combined project of my poetry and photographs that I had created when I was fifteen, the same age as my daughter. I sat reading these very existential poems with tears in my eyes, flooded with memories.

On a whim I called my daughter to come join me in the

basement. She came down and immediately squealed with delight at the old record albums. (The Beatles, Creedence Clearwater Revival, Jefferson Airplane—you name it, I had it.) She rummaged through my ancient possessions as though she had discovered buried treasure, exclaiming how excited Becky, her best friend, would be when she brought them home.

Then I took a chance and showed her my sacred project, which was dog-eared and slightly discolored from age. She sat intently staring at the black-and-white photographs and reading the accompanying poems. I felt as if I were waiting for a review from *The New York Times*. Finally she looked up at me and said, "Mom this is rad. Can we take it home with us? Do you still have any of the negatives around?" We dug into another box, and there was my old plastic shoe box filled with carefully labeled negatives. "Maybe I can make some proof sheets from these in photography class," Ama offered. I was moved and delighted by her receptivity and interest.

On the drive home from the airport Ama was silent for a long time before she commented. "This trip was great," she said finally. "You seemed more like me."

When we share something that is meaningful for us, we invite a deeper level of connectedness and relating with our kids. It strengthens our bond when we let them into our world, by sharing a poem, a favorite piece of music, a special seashell, or a story that we found particularly moving. They are able to see us as fuller human beings.

Getting to Know You

There is nothing as precious as stepping out of the role of parent and into the role of friend from time to time, and getting to know your child as a person.

Take time to ask your children's opinions about everything from the everyday aspects of life to more global issues: "Where do you think we should go on our vacation?" "What color do you think we should paint the family room?" "What do you think about the tension in the Middle East?" "How do you feel about homeless people?" "If you were the President, what would you do about the environment?" You may be amazed at the wisdom of your children. Kids appreciate having parents who listen to and respect their thoughts and opinions—even when they differ from our own.

Listening Equals Love

Things happen to our children that may seem trivial and unimportant to us, but are of major importance to them. Put yourself in their shoes and show them that you genuinely value what they share with you. Ask them about school, their friends, and their interests every day. Become an interested listener in their lives. Show them that you care enough to hear their stories and struggles, and they will interpret this to mean that they themselves are significant. For your kids, their relationships with their friends are of utmost importance. Later their appearance and peer approval take precedence. It may sound trivial to you, but it's their world, and earthshakingly important to them.

5. TOUCH EACH OTHER

When you fall in love with someone, you hug and touch constantly. Children also need to be touched and hugged on a more regular basis. Virginia Satir has a prescription for touching:

Four hugs a day for survival, eight for maintenance, and sixteen for growth. If you want your kids to thrive, make sure that they get hugged a lot.

We may prepare food for our children, chauffeur them around, take them to the movies, buy them toys and ice cream, but nothing registers as deeply as a simple squeeze, cuddle, or pat on the back. There is no greater reassurance of their lovability and worth than to be affectionately touched and held. By giving our kids appropriate physical contact, we send them into the world with renewed inner strength to cope with the multitude of challenges they face daily.

Dr. René Spitz published his classic study in 1946 of a phenomenon he called failure-to-thrive syndrome. He was working in a hospital for abandoned infants and toddlers whose mothers were in prison. He became alarmed when he discovered that while the infants had been well fed and kept in highly sanitary conditions, they suffered a high degree of deaths from what is called "marasmus," meaning a wasting away or shriveling up without any apparent medical cause.

While vacationing in Mexico, Spitz visited another orphanage, in which the conditions were less sanitary, but where the babies seemed happier, healthier, and more alert, and cried less. In trying to discover the difference, he observed that women from the village came every day to the Mexican hospital and held and rocked the babies, talking and singing to them.

In his subsequent studies of thousands of babies he observed that babies who are touched thrive, while those who are left alone in bassinets tend to become ill, suffering from what Spitz called skin hunger—i.e., a lack of physical contact.[4]

Children need to be touched for their emotional survival. They are never too old to get a hug. They change and mature, yes, but they never lose that need. My daughter still loves me to hug her (and even tickle her now and then, if her friends aren't around).

Oddly, many parents rely more than they are aware on words to convey their love and affection to their children. In research done by two psychologists at the University of Pittsburgh in which they observed families on the beaches of Greece, the Soviet Union, and the United States, they noticed that when it came to punishing or retrieving children, the amount of touch was very similar. But when it came to soothing, holding, and play, American children received *significantly less contact* than those of the other cultures.[5]

We need to combine both verbal and nonverbal messages in communicating our good feelings and love for our children. Holding your son's hand, gently stroking your daughter's face, hugging, and kissing, often speak louder than our words.

Incidentally you can amplify the benefit of touching by telling your children how much you appreciate the physical affection you share together. A father in one of my classes reported that he said to his son, "I really like when we cuddle on the couch and read stories together." Still another parent reported that she was able to encourage more physical contact from her kids when after spontaneous hugs she began saying, "Thanks for the hug. I feel good!"

Try a Little Tenderness

Some of the most effective loving touching really just comes under the heading of tenderness. We are tender toward our animals, our gardens, our cars, and our jewelry, yet we are often so hard on ourselves and our children.

Tenderness doesn't take any extra time, and can be easily given while other activities are going on. As you walk through your house, you can gently pat your child on the back as you pass by. It takes no extra time to gently stroke your child's face as you are scrambling to get off to work in the morning. As you place your children's breakfast in front of them, you can press your hand on theirs at the same time or touch them on the back of the neck while they are sitting at the table. What it conveys is, "I'm glad you're here."

There are numerous ways to show how much we mean to one another. We have a marvelous opportunity literally at our fingertips to promote a sense of emotional security in our children. These small gestures we make carry significant meaning.

Equality of Touch

Research shows that girl infants less than a year old receive five times as much physical affection as boy babies. Boys need to be held, cuddled, hugged, and kissed every bit as much as girls do, especially as young children. Moreover, although early childhood may be the most crucial period for affection, both boys and girls never outgrow the need for physical contact.

Unfortunately, there is still a cultural stereotype that it's all right for girls to be affectionate but that once boys reach six or seven, they no longer need so much hugging and kissing. What this does is dissuade boys from expressing their natural feelings of tenderness and affection. It is important that we act affectionately with our sons as well as our daughters. The style of affection might change to include back-slapping, bear hugs, and high fives (hand-slapping). But, people of all ages need to be touched. It's part of being human.

A friend of mine has raised two young men, Gene, twenty-two, and Darrell, nineteen. I was at their house having dinner recently, and Gene came in with his girlfriend. He walked into the room, came over to his mother and father, and gave each of them a warm hug. It was as natural to him as saying hello. Gene was raised with a lot of physical expression of affection, and is comfortable with physical contact.

Research done at UCLA states that "hugging relieves many physical and emotional problems and can help people live longer, maintain health, relieve stress, and promote sleep."

"Hugging is an excellent tonic," declares Dr. Harold Voth, senior psychiatrist at the Menninger Foundation. "Hugging breathes new life into a tired body and makes you feel younger and more vibrant. In the home, daily hugging will strengthen relationships and significantly reduce friction."[6]

If you want your children to have high self-esteem, then you need to hug and touch them every day.

6. TELL YOUR CHILDREN OFTEN THAT YOU LOVE THEM

When I ask parents if they tell their children that they love them, the answer I often get is, "No, but they know that I do." Children need to be told directly and often, "I love you." I've never had anyone come up to me at the end of a seminar and say, "Could you please tell my husband to stop telling me he loves me!" We can never hear "I love you" too often.

Our children don't automatically feel loved simply because they are our children. They need tangible demonstrations of your loving.

We can use affirming statements to express our love to our children, such as "I love you just the way you are. I'm so glad you're my daughter!" These kinds of affirming messages need to be given to your children day in and day out for the rest of their lives. Researchers were surprised to find in repeated studies that these reassuring messages have a measurably calming and nurturing effect even on infants. By continually affirming our children's lovableness and capableness, we foster the development of a strong sense of self. The more love you give your children, the more love you are helping them create inside themselves. Think of love as a basic birthright of your kids. Give it away freely, and it will come back a thousandfold.[7]

Terms of Endearment

If you are uncomfortable saying "I love you" directly, or if you'd like an alternative way of expressing affection, use humor. Tell your four-year-old you love him bigger than the ocean and higher than the sky. You can also make up terms of endearment or pet names. Or use the familiar ones, such as sugarplum, honey pie, sweetie, boobie, toots, scootie, lovie. Have fun in the process!

7. TREAT YOUR CHILDREN AS IF THEY ARE THE MOST IMPORTANT PEOPLE IN THE WORLD

Most of us say things to our kids that we wouldn't say to anyone else. Ask yourself, If you treated your friends the way you treat your kids, would you have any left?

We need to treat our children with love, respect, and understanding if that's how we want them to treat us, others, and most important, themselves. Although our children deserve the same kind of respect and consideration we would give to an adult friend, we often treat our kids like second-class citizens. We talk down to them, embarrass them, order them around, and generally treat them disrespectfully. Even when we don't intend to, we build barriers between ourselves and our children instead of bridges. Every time we criticize, embarrass, or order them around, we cement another brick into the wall. If we continue to treat them in this way, they will eventually shut us out because they have experienced too much hurt.

GIVE ME YOUR UNCONDITIONAL LOVE

Our kids shouldn't have to earn our love, acceptance, or respect. These are your child's birthright and should be given freely. If children are only accepted and loved when they do what we expect or what we want, they feel insecure and never really feel that they are genuinely loved and valued.

Respect and acceptance don't mean you accept or like everything they do, but that you love them no matter what.

Unconditional love is loving your kids for who they *are*, not for what they *do*. Unfortunately many parents love their kids if they get good grades, clean their rooms, make the all-star team, or get elected class president. This kind of love is conditional.

Children who receive conditional love don't feel that they deserve love but that they have to earn it. They learn that love is tied to performance.

Kids who feel that they have to earn love are headed for trouble. A teenager I was seeing in counseling once said to me after a suicide attempt, "If my parents don't even love me, why should I love myself?" The feeling that "I am unlovable unless I do what you want, and I am nothing if I don't" is devastating.

Unconditional love is loving your child no matter what. That means regardless of how he looks or what his talents, deficits, or handicaps may be. Unconditional love means loving your kids—and this means regardless of what we expect them to be and (the most difficult one) no matter how they act. By this, I don't mean that we like or accept inappropriate behavior, but with unconditional love we love the child even at those times when we dislike his or her behavior.

Unconditional love isn't something you will achieve every minute of every day. But it is the thought we must hold in our hearts every day. The underlying message of unconditional love is, "I love you no matter what you do. I am committed to you one hundred percent. And will be here for you through thick or thin."

Dr. Gerald Jampolsky, in his book *Teach Only Love*, puts it well. "True love," he writes, "is a completely pure and unencumbered form of giving. It is extended freely to the love in others and is its own reward."[8]

8. CREATE LASTING MEMORIES

In a survey done of fifteen thousand schoolchildren the question was asked, "What do you think makes a happy family?" When the kids answered, they didn't list a big house, fancy cars, or new video games as the source of happiness. The most frequently given answer was "doing things together."[9]

The most basic need that children have is to feel that they belong. In infancy a child's very existence and survival is based on belonging. As children develop and grow, their sense of belonging to a group enhances their emotional and psychological health.

ALL TOGETHER NOW

Melinda described one of her family traditions in a session we had together. "Every summer we rent a camper," she said, "and Tom and the kids and I all pile in and head up the coast to the beach. We have our favorite spot that we've been going to for the past eight years now, and we all love it. On the drive up the coast there is a special beach we always stop at to collect treasures. We call it Coya Beach. And that's the name we've given to the treasures we find there. Then we drive another hour up the coast to our campsite and settle in. We all have a wonderful time, and the kids look forward to it every year."

By creating family traditions and rituals, you provide your children with a sense of continuity. After your kids leave home, they will continue to have a strong sense of belonging when they think back on certain family traditions.

In my seminars I ask parents to do an exercise I call "Recalling Happy Memories." I ask people to take a few minutes and drift back through their childhoods, and recall the happiest times they spent with their families. Then I ask people to share some of their happiest memories. The results are always delightfully varied:

> "I remember Sunday mornings with everyone sitting in the family room eating bagels and lox, listening to classical music with my parents reading the Sunday paper."

> "Having my mom and dad tuck me in at night and reading me stories."

"Going on a camping trip and my dad telling ghost stories around the campfire at night and my brother and I getting so scared we slept in the same sleeping bag that night."

"Family circles. That was a family gathering of all our cousins and relatives at my grandparents' house for a big dinner. The grown-ups would sit and talk about family business, and we would play hide-and-seek in my grandparents' house."

"On Halloween my dad would dress up like Dracula and we would build a haunted house on our porch with spiderwebs and scary sounds. The kids would have to go through it to get their candy."

As different as these happy memories are on the surface, what they all have in common is the warmth of a family doing something special together.

As a family, take time to discuss the family traditions you already have and what new ones you would like to establish. Write down your ideas and then put them on a family calendar. Sometimes that's all it takes to get you started.

In one family I worked with, James, an eight-year-old, didn't feel as if his family ever did anything together. He was one of three children, and part of the problem was deciding on what to do that everybody would participate in. So we devised a system in which everyone could choose one thing he really wanted to do with the understanding that all the other family members would participate, regardless of their interest level. Then James sat down and made a family calendar on which he scheduled the new family events. James picked playing soccer. Lydia wanted to go ride the carousel. Danny wanted to go bowling. Mom wanted to have a picnic, and Dad wanted to take a hike. Over a seven-week period James and his family were able to complete each one of the chosen activities. This turned out to be so much fun, they decided to incorporate the "activity calendar" into their regular family routine.

9. CELEBRATE UNIQUENESS

Our children thrive when they know that the important people in their lives recognize their uniqueness. They learn to feel unique through the way they are treated. This helps them to form their sense of individuality. Children's uniqueness blossoms when they feel cared for. Time spent taking care of our children contributes to their feelings of safety, security, and uniqueness.

In his book *The Little Prince* Antoine de Saint Exupéry wonderfully illustrates the connections between dedication, caring, and specialness. The Little Prince comes to visit earth from a distant planet. On his home planet he has a special rose, which he leaves behind in order to explore the vast universe. In the course of his adventures on earth he encounters a field of roses and, for a moment, he doubts that his rose is indeed special since here are so many beautiful roses. But in time, he realizes the difference. "You are not like my rose," he says finally to the earth roses. "As yet you are nothing. No one has tamed you, and you have tamed no one. You are like my fox when I first knew him. He was only a fox like a hundred thousand other foxes. But I have made him my friend, and now he is unique in all the world." And the roses were very much embarrassed. "You are beautiful, but you are empty," he goes on. "One could not die for you. To be sure, an ordinary passerby would think that my rose looked just like you—the rose that belongs to me. But in herself alone she is more important than all the hundreds of you other roses: because it is she that I have watered; because it is she that I have put under a glass globe; because it is she that I have sheltered behind the screen; because it is for her that I have killed the caterpillars (except the two or three that we saved to become butterflies); because it is she that I have listened to, when she grumbled, or boasted,

FALLING IN LOVE WITH YOUR KIDS

or even sometimes when she said nothing. Because she is *my* rose."

. . . Then the Little Prince went back to say good-bye to his friend the fox and the fox said, "And now here is my secret, a very simple secret: It is only with the heart that one can see rightly; what is essential is invisible to the eye. . . . It is the time you have wasted for your rose that makes your rose so important. . . . Men have forgotten this truth."[10]

The time, care, and sacrifices the Little Prince made for his rose secured her uniqueness in his heart. The more of himself he invested in her, the more unique and precious she became.

Spending time and caring for our children does make them more precious and special to us and more special to themselves. We develop a unique relationship that is strengthened by time and a shared sense of history.

Did you know that with all the millions of people on this earth, there is no one exactly like you? There is no one with the same combination of eyes, hair, facial features; with the same hopes, fears, concerns, dreams; with the same genes and chromosomes. And with billions of people yet to be born, there will never be anyone just like you. You're unique, special, and one-of-a-kind. This is also true for each of your children.

For a long time I expected my daughter to be athletic because athletics was one of my strong interests as a kid. I kept pushing her into organized sports, and would get frustrated and angry with her when she resisted. Finally it dawned on me that Ama wasn't me, and that she doesn't have the exact same interests or talents that I did. In fact, she is very artistic and creative, and loves art and dance. Her unique expression is different from mine, and equally valuable and wonderful. Once I recognized Ama's uniqueness, life became a lot easier.

I'd like to give you five projects you can do with your children to help them realize that they are unique. Each can be adapted to the various ages of your kids.

Project #1. Making a Commercial

Ask your children to write a TV commercial about themselves. Start with a storyboard, which is a series of boxes containing pictures and words. With really young children, let them draw the pictures while you take down the dialogue or narration. What we know about commercials is that they never say anything bad about the product. They only sing its praises and tell you its good points. Your children will also focus solely on the positive in their commercials. As kids participate, they start to think about everything good about themselves. Families who have used this project have reported to me that their children loved to act their commercials out after dinner at a special talent hour.

After each child has made a commercial, you can make a family commercial. What makes your family special? What are your family's unique characteristics? Get another sheet of paper and make a storyboard and create another commercial. You can display the storyboards in a prominent spot like the family art gallery (the refrigerator).

Project #2. An "I Am Special and Loved" Poster

Take an 8 1/2" by 11" piece of paper and attach a photo of your child at the top. Beneath the heading "I am special and loved" have your children describe their bodies using as many adjectives as possible. "I have brown curly hair with long bangs." If you have identical twins, have each child include special experiences and accomplishments. When they get finished, especially if you have more than one child, you'll find they come to the marvelous realization that no one looks exactly the way they do, no one has eyes just like theirs. They will recognize that they are unique and don't look like their brother, or their uncle Fred, or anyone else.

Project #3. Scrapbooks

Scrapbooks are great. Kids love to save pictures from their childhood, special cards, letters, awards, things they feel proud of. It gives them a way to look back on their history and see where they came from and things that they accomplished. Scrapbooks give kids a sense of time and a love of history that may even translate into better scholastic performance.

Project #4. "My Special Box"

This is particularly good for young children. The Special Box can be a cardboard box or a shoe box, or it can be fancier than that. When I was about eight years old, my grandfather gave me a beautifully decorated cigar box. He was a grocer, and got lots of neat boxes and containers. I placed it on my dresser, and that box became a place I could put things. A couple of years ago I went back to my parents' house for Thanksgiving and was snooping around in their attic, and I found my special box.

If I showed it to you, you'd look at it and say, "Looks like junk." But to me it was the treasure chest of my childhood. It had my ponytail that I got cut off when I went to first grade, my baby teeth, my half of the friendship heart that my best friend Dale Seiden had given me. I had birthday cards, merit badges from Girl Scouts, and a special letter from my favorite uncle. To this day I treasure it.

Project #5. Photos

Whether or not your family is big on taking pictures, I'd like to suggest that each of your children have two pictures next to his or her bed. One should show him happy while doing something. He could be riding a bike, playing softball, painting, or baking. The other photo should show your family together.

Why put them next to their beds? Research has shown that there is a thirty-minute time period each day when your children are more receptive—thirty minutes when they will listen to you and absorb more than at any other time. That thirty minutes is the period just before your children go to bed. Unfortunately 95 percent of American kids watch TV during this critical time.

If you put photos of your kids being capable and loved next to their beds, these positive visual images are likely to be the last thing they see before they sleep and the first thing they see when they awaken. Consequently the message "I am lovable and capable," the two keys to high self-esteem, will be strengthened even while your children are asleep. Why does this work? Here's the amazing thing: Studies show that during sleep the subconscious will review what has been recorded all day, between three to five times. But it will replay what has been recorded in the last thirty minutes before we go to sleep *at least ten times*. Those two pictures next to the bed are one way of making sure that "I am lovable and capable" gets reinforced ten times over rather than *Friday the 13th, part 27*.

Those five projects are great to do with and for your kids. Here's an exercise to remind yourself that each member of your family is special.

MY FAMILY IS SPECIAL

1. Which is the child with whom you have the most friction?

2. What is unique and special about this child?

3. List at least three things that are unique about every one in your family.

Your Spouse: (name)_____

1. _____

2. _____

3. _____

Your first number one: (name)_____

1. _____

2. _____

3. _____

Your first number two: (name)_____

1. _____

2. _____

3. _____

Your first number three: (name)_____

1. _____

2. _____

3. _____

Yourself: (name)_____

1. _____

2. _____

3. _____

Tonight at the dinner table or at bedtime I'd like you to share what you think is special about each of your family members with them. It changes the quality of your interactions when you talk about and celebrate your children's uniqueness. As we start to recognize and express their uniqueness, our children will grow to value themselves more.

Our children need to be loved so completely that they learn

to love themselves. Children who feel loved know, accept, and like who they are and have a strong sense of self-esteem. They act responsibly and have a generally positive attitude about life.

Take the time to get to know your children and to enjoy them. It will add new dimensions to parenting.

Here's one final exercise that helps the entire family express love more freely.

HEART SHARINGS

Heart sharings are based on the Hopi Indian tradition of the talking stick. Tribe members would gather in their sacred ceremonial room called a *kiva* to have council meetings. The meeting was structured in such a way that each person would have an opportunity to speak while having the focused attention of everyone present. The way this was done was that a special stick was passed from person to person. The rule was that the person holding the stick had the floor, and was not to be interrupted while speaking.

Over time this ritual has evolved. Now, sometimes a pipe is used, other times a feather. I have used heart sharings in families by passing a teddy bear, a piece of wood, or a seashell. You can use any object. What's important is that the object represents speaking from your heart with love, honesty, and compassion.

The purpose of heart sharings is for each person to have a chance to say what is in their hearts, openly and with the full attention of all the other family members. You can plan a heart sharing about a specific issue, or use it as a regular time for family sharing. This builds a structured time when everyone in your family—from the youngest child to the parents—can share any grievances, hopes, concerns, appreciations, discuss a particular issue, or make a family decision.

Here are the guidelines for having a heart sharing:

1. Only the person with the special object talks. Everyone else listens with full attention and support.
2. Pass the object gently to the left to the next person. Do not throw it.
3. Anyone can choose not to share. Just pass the object to the next person.
4. Talk about what *you* feel or think, not about what someone else said.
5. Listen fully, without planning what you are going to say. Avoid criticism, advice, or opinions.
6. Create an atmosphere of safety in which to share. Make a confidentiality pact to not tell anyone else what someone has shared.
7. Be thoughtful of how long you speak so everyone can have a turn (or you can set a time limit—each person will have three minutes or whatever).

Exercise: Showing Your Love

Take a moment and ask yourself what situation made you feel loved as a child?

Who were you with?

How did you feel about yourself?

How did you feel about them?

What were they doing that communicated their love to you?

What are you currently doing to communicate your love to your children?

Exercise: Bedtime Ritual

Share your happiest moment of the day and your saddest time during the day.

Then ask your children to tell you theirs. Share something you did today that you feel good about, and again ask them to share something with you as well.

I have suggested the following format to parents in my seminars for family meetings to precede the heart sharings:

1. Start the meeting by asking if anyone has any news to share or information to communicate to the family, such as "Mom will be going out of town next week on a business trip," or "Aunt Susan will be coming to dinner tomorrow night."

2. Ask if anyone has any complaints, bugs, or irritations. The rule about stating a complaint is it must be accompanied by a recommendation for change. The idea is that the person who has the complaint is the resource for the solution. Cathy: "It bugs me that there is never anything good to eat in this house." Mother: "What is your suggestion?" Cathy: "I think we should make a list of what we want so you can take it to the market when you go shopping."

3. Next ask for any hopes or wishes for the future. This allows people to voice their wishes without necessarily expecting that the wish will be fulfilled.

4. And finally appreciations, a very neglected area of our lives. This allows people to say what they like, love, and appreciate about one another. "I appreciate the way Benny put his clothes in the laundry this week." This initial process sets the stage and tone for the heart sharing. You can continue by either having an open heart sharing or by choosing a specific topic, such as:

- The biggest challenge you are currently facing is . . .
- Something you do well is . . .
- Something you like about yourself is . . .
- What is the best thing that ever happened to you? Why?
- When you make a mistake you feel . . .
- If you could trade places with anyone else in the world for a day, who would you be? Why?
- If you could change anything about yourself, what would you change? Why?
- If you had three wishes, what would you wish for? Explain why you want each one. What would make you feel happier than you are now?

Chapter 4
THE MAGIC OF ENCOURAGEMENT

"Children need encouragement, just as plants need water. They cannot survive without it."
—Rudolph Dreikurs [1]

"What a slob. Your room is a pigsty. You're such a klutz. What on earth is wrong with you? Can't you do anything right! How stupid can you get? Bad girl! What did I ever do to deserve a kid like you? You're impossible! Just wait until you have kids of your own. Talking to you is like talking to a brick wall. You never think of anyone but yourself. At the rate you're going, you're never going to amount to anything!"

All of these phrases are forms of criticism. This chapter is about encouragement. But first we're going to look at encouragement's polar opposite: criticism.

THE SLEDGEHAMMER EFFECT OF CRITICISM

There is one thing that can undermine all the hard self-esteem building we do, and that is verbal criticism. When we criticize our children we believe that we are doing them a favor. We are "helping" them by identifying their inappropriate behavior so that they can mend the error of their ways and become happier, more successful people. Right?

The truth is that criticism from our parents didn't work that way with us, and it certainly doesn't work that way with our own kids. Like a sledgehammer on a priceless vase, criticism in any form makes shards out of our kids' confidence and motivation to try something new. It incites either rebellion, resentment, or resignation, because they take what we say about them very personally. Criticism is never "constructive" because it strips our children of their precious sense of dignity and self-worth.

A study from the University of Calgary shows that verbal abuse is even more likely than physical abuse to damage children's self-esteem.[2]

Our children evaluate themselves based on the opinions we have of them. When we use harsh words, biting comments, and a sarcastic tone of voice we plant the seeds of self-doubt in their developing minds. The underlying messages associated with criticism are "You're incompetent and unlovable, and who you are isn't enough." Children who receive a steady diet of these types of messages end up feeling powerless, inadequate, and unimportant. They start to believe that they *are* bad, and that they can never do enough. Consequently, their self-esteem begins to crumble.

BAD BERTHA

Some days I have this image of myself sitting on top of the refrigerator waiting for my daughter to come in. I have a pair of binoculars, a pad, and a pencil, and take note of all the things she did wrong or failed to do: "You forgot to take out the garbage, your room is a mess. You left your book bag in the hallway. You didn't put your dishes in the sink!" Then I watch her crawl into her shell and withdraw, or come back at me ready to engage in mortal combat.

THE SAME OLD SONG

You may be shocked if you really stop to listen to the words that come out of your mouth. I can remember standing in the kitchen and lashing out at my daughter, "What a pig! You never put anything away." Suddenly I was dumbstruck when I realized that the very words I hated hearing as a child and had sworn never to utter were exactly the words I was spewing forth in tones of righteous indignation. We are often unaware that we are replaying the old tapes from our childhood for our children's ears.

Cynthia, a mother in one of my seminars, reported that she was flooded with memories of how discouraged she felt by the negative labeling she experienced as a child. "I was called stupid so often," she confided, "that even now, as a grown woman, I continually struggle with a critical internal voice that repeatedly says, 'You're stupid, and you'll never amount to anything.'" Cynthia has a master's degree in business administration, a very successful career, and a solid marriage. But she is still plagued by those early messages. "It's taught me how important it is to monitor what I say to my own children," Cynthia says now. "I'm so conscious of the need to focus on their strengths and attributes instead of nitpicking them to death."

(I suggested that she create an antidote statement to those poisonous early messages, like, "I am an intelligent, worthwhile, and loving woman." She now repeats this silently to herself whenever she hears the old tape click on.)

CRITICISM LEAVES A LASTING IMPRESSION

Jack Canfield cites a study done at the University of Iowa. A group of graduate students followed around normal two-year-olds for a day. What they observed at the end of the day was that the children were continually inundated with negative nudge statements, such as "Don't touch the vase, you'll break it," "Bad boy," "No, you're not big enough to try that." The average kids from average families received 432 negative statements as opposed to 32 positive acknowledgments *daily*. That is a ratio of 13.5 to 1.[3] The national average according to a study done by the National Parent-Teachers Organization of parent-to-child criticism versus praise is 18 to 1. That's eighteen critical messages to every compliment. What kind of effect do you think such a steady diet of criticism has on a child? What effect would it have on you as an adult?

Before you answer, let me tell you about a correlating study done with a woman who was eight months pregnant. She was attached to a fetal heart monitor and was given a script to read. The first script went like this: "I can't wait to have this baby. It's such a wonderful time to be having it. We have the room all fixed up and the crib ready and are so looking forward to having a child. I can't wait for the baby to be born." The research team measured the fetal heart rate once as she read and noted that it increased four beats per minute. After her heart rate returned to normal, they had her then read a different script: "It's really not a good time for us to be having this baby. We need two incomes to make it. If I didn't have this baby, I could progress in my career. This isn't a good time for me to give birth." The researchers measured the heart rate once again. It went *down* four beats per minute. If what we think and say affects even an unborn baby, what is it doing to our developing children? Our words are very powerful, especially with such impressionable minds. We need to stop and consider the impact of our words on our children.

THERE'S NO SUCH THING AS A BAD KID

So how do we correct misbehavior without criticizing? The first key to remember is this: When your children misbehave, as they inevitably will, you *point to the behavior rather than to the child.* Separate the child from the behavior: "I love you, I don't like what you did." We can talk about what they did that was inappropriate without attacking them personally. I'll give you some examples:

Critical Statement	*Focus on Misbehavior*
"You're so selfish."	"I hate it when you don't call and tell me where you are."
"You're a slob."	"This mess really bothers me, please clean it up."
"What are you, stupid? You know your report is due tomorrow."	"I feel frustrated when you don't plan your time better. I'd like you to make your schoolwork a priority."

When we use "you" followed by a noun or an adjective that describes our children we are passing judgment. In most cases using "I" followed by our reaction or feeling sends a message directed toward our kids' *behavior,* not toward the children themselves. When we sit in judgment of our children, we are asking for trouble because they take what we say about who they are as the gospel truth.

ENCOURAGEMENT VS. CRITICISM

Psychologist/author Michael Popkin tells this story: I'd like you to take a moment and imagine yourself in this situation. You're driving home from work, and suddenly you notice in your rearview mirror that a police car is following you with the red and yellow lights flashing. You check your speedometer and notice that you are driving right at the speed limit. As your pulse begins to race, you curse under your breath and wonder what you did wrong. You notice your sweaty palms as you pull over, and the police officer walks up to your car. You roll down your window, and he asks to see your license.

He examines it and says, "I've been on the police force for fifteen years, and I have never in my life seen such a considerate, careful driver. Back there at the overpass you maneuvered through that snarl skillfully, courteously, and never honked your horn once. If there were more courteous drivers like you, my job would be a lot easier. I just had to tell you that, and say thanks."

If this happened to you, what would your first reaction be? Shock, disbelief, anger? "Who's this guy kidding? Is this some kind of joke? He hauled me over for *that*?" We don't expect authority figures to give us compliments. Starting with our parents, and continuing through teachers and supervisors, we have come to expect criticism, ridicule, and reprimands rather than encouragement, support and praise. But admit it: After your pulse returns to normal and the shock has worn off, you'd probably feel good about yourself and your driving skills. And I'd bet that you'd find yourself acting even more courteously in the future. I know I would.[4]

Popkin's story of the police officer is a perfect example of the magic of encouragement. If only a few words from a perfect stranger could increase your self-esteem and confidence, and create the probability that you would drive even better in the future, imagine the effect our encouragement can have on our children.

Praise is such a wonderful tool. All you have to do is to start catching your children doing things right and comment on these actions. Their behavior may not change immediately, but they will start to do more of what you notice and focus on. When we express appreciation, we support our kids in repeating the appropriate behavior. No matter how it may look, they really do want to cooperate. And, like us, they're not mind readers: We need to tell them specifically how best to please us.

THE FINE ART OF PRAISE

Praising your child is the simplest thing in the world. Right? Wrong. Praise is both a magic wand and a weapon. Used correctly, it supports children in feeling confident, capable, and secure. But praise used incorrectly can result in anxiety, insecurity, and misbehavior. I'll show you what I mean:

Celeste comes running into the house madly waving her report card. She flings open the envelope and rushes over to show her parents. Celeste has gotten three "A"s, two "B"s, and a "C" in science. As her parents look it over, her father says, "What's this 'C' in science? You can do better than that. There's no excuse for such a poor grade."

Okay, this is not praise. This is negative feedback. You can see how Celeste would feel bad about herself and think that she is unworthy of her parents' acknowledgment and approval when they focus their attention on the one "C" rather than the other grades.

However, Randy's situation is less obvious. Randy arrives home with the exact same report card as Celeste, but his parents focus on the "A"s he received in English, history, and math. "Randy, you're so smart. We're so proud of you. You're a real genius. I bet next time you'll get *all* 'A's."

In Randy's case the praise his parents gave was ineffective

on two counts. First, it burdened him with extremely high expectations, too high for him to live up to comfortably. Second, the praise focused on *him* rather than his *efforts*: "You're so smart . . . you're a real genius." This sends a confusing message to kids. They are likely to worry: "If my parents can call me a genius now, what happens if I bring home all 'C's next marking period? Will they call me dumb?" Kids will wonder if their parents will appreciate and care for them less if they perform poorly.

THE LANGUAGE OF ENCOURAGEMENT

So what do you do instead? Offer your enthusiasm and encouragement in the form of descriptive praise. (I am going to use the words "encouragement" and "descriptive praise" interchangeably.)

When using encouragement, we need to describe and appreciate our kids' efforts without judgment or evaluation. In Randy's case, his parents might have said, "I can see from your report card that you really hit the books this semester. I bet you feel good about yourself." This kind of response not only acknowledges Randy's determination and effort, but it also lets him know that his parents understand his feelings. By mirroring your children's good feelings, you communicate your caring and demonstrate that you are paying attention to them.

Descriptive praise focuses on the deed, not the doer. Unlike ineffective praise, encouragement does not evaluate a child's efforts or achievements. Phrases like "You're an angel" or "You're terrific!," if used exclusively, are too general and set unrealistic standards for our kids to live up to. These types of comments focus on the child's character rather than on her effort or accomplishments. Instead of using words that evaluate, describe in concrete terms what you see and how you feel. "I appreciate you sharing your trucks." "Thanks for calling when you knew you were going to be late."

Guidelines for the Fine Art of Praise

1. Focus on your child's efforts and achievements, not on his character. For example, rather than saying, "You're a terrific kid," you might say, "I really appreciate your help bringing in the groceries."
2. Be specific in your praise. Rather than "You're doing a good job," say, "I like the way you got dressed all by yourself this morning." Your child is clear about what the specific behavior is that you want more of.
3. Tell your children how you feel about what they did. "I was touched by the card you sent me." "I appreciate your thoughtfulness."
4. Your comments should encourage your children to draw positive conclusions about themselves. "I appreciate when you water the garden." Child's interpretation: "I am helpful."
6. Focus on your child's efforts and progress. "Skating a mile! Hey, you couldn't do that two weeks ago!" "You studied really hard for the math final, and it really paid off."
7. Once you've given the praise, stop talking for a few moments to allow your child to take it in. Then give him a hug!

Below are several examples to help you see the contrast between effective praise and the conclusions your child might make:

Effective praise: "I appreciate it when you put your toys away. You really stacked everything neatly."
Child's conclusions: "I'm responsible and can take care of my things."

Effective praise: "I love the tie you picked out for Grandpa's birthday. I think he will really like it."

Child's conclusions: "I have good taste and can make other people happy."

Effective praise: "I love the way your mobile hangs and moves in the breeze. It's fun to look at it."
Child's conclusions: "I can be creative and original."[5]

By appreciating your children's efforts you encourage a repeat performance. Your children need to know what's expected of them to feel capable of being successful. When your kids hear these positive messages, they internalize them and they later become part of their nurturing internal dialogue. Through this process your children develop the ability to recognize and appreciate their own strengths and abilities.

Kids thrive in an environment where they aren't afraid of being evaluated and judged. Encouragement fosters independence, self-esteem, a willingness to explore and experiment, plus an acceptance for self and others. Our effective praise should be a way of celebrating our kids rather than evaluating them. Your actions and words let your kids know that you are glad that they are who they are.

FIVE KEYS TO USING ENCOURAGEMENT

Now, I'd like to teach you five ways to use encouragement to create higher self-esteem in your children:

1. Build on your children's strengths by catching them doing something right.
2. Express appreciation when your children are cooperative and helpful.
3. Give positive support for each step along the way to achieving a goal or new behavior.
4. Show confidence.
5. Nurture success.

Let me explain in more detail:

1. BUILD ON YOUR CHILDREN'S STRENGTHS

Catch your children doing something right and comment on it. We spend so much of our time focusing on what isn't working and on what they are doing wrong. We take on the role of Ms. and Mr. Fixit and feel obliged to look for problems and then to come up with the solutions. Start to shift your attention to notice what they are doing right. Nurturing competence, the food of self-esteem, comes from acknowledging and appreciating the positive contributions your children make. By catching our kids doing things right, we bring out the good that is already there.

"I really appreciated the way you sat quietly while we were in the dentist's office."

"I like the way you put your toys away today."

"Thanks for clearing the table tonight. It was a big help."

What you see is what you get. When we spend our time focusing on the negative, it grows. On the other hand, if we focus our time, attention, and energy on the positive, it won't be long before the negative decreases and the positive increases. It's very encouraging to yourself and to your children when you focus on what's working.

Have You Praised Your Kids Today?

Sometimes exasperated parents say to me, "Praise my child? You must be kidding! He doesn't do anything right!" When this is how a parent is feeling, I suggest that they start with the one-a-day technique developed by parent educator Nancy Samalin.[6] Praise one good thing your child has done, no matter how small or insignificant it may be: "Ashley, I see you tied your shoes all by yourself." "Your sister must appreciate it when you help her ride her bike. She's lucky to have you as her brother."

If you use the one-a-day technique, I guarantee that within a week you will notice that your child has begun to do more praiseworthy things. When your child is having a difficult time, it is especially important that you find something he did right and let him know that you liked it. Start even with the small things and watch them grow.

Exercise in praise: Set a goal for yourself of giving at least one compliment per day to each of your family members. At first it may seem mechanical, but in time it will become second nature.

2. EXPRESS APPRECIATION WHEN YOUR CHILDREN ARE HELPFUL AND COOPERATIVE

Everyone wants to feel appreciated. We want to feel valued for who we are and what we do. When we express appreciation to our children, what we are saying is, "You are a worthwhile and important person. I'm interested in you and recognize your positive qualities." That is a pretty powerful message.

Don't take children's efforts for granted. Even when our children do their assigned chores, it helps to notice and to appreciate their cooperation.

"You sure helped me by making the salad tonight."

"It's fun to read to you when you sit quietly and listen to me."

"I appreciated your playing quietly while I took a rest."

What Goes Around Comes Around

Cameron, a mother in one of my advanced seminars, had an interesting observation after several weeks of working with her praise techniques: "You know," she said, "I noticed that my oldest son, Ryan, is starting to thank *me* and compliment *me* more. I guess this stuff rubs off if we are sincere in expressing our appreciation and we do it consistently enough!"

Yes, our children can learn to express appreciation as well. Children learn by example. If we give regular messages of appreciation to one another and to our kids, they will develop this wonderful habit. Their awareness can start out simply through being reminded to say thank you.

I still get a warm feeling every time my daughter says, "Thanks for dinner, Mom." Or, "Thanks for taking me to my friend's house." Appreciation is the one gift nobody ever gets tired of receiving over and over again.

The Ultimate Test

Cecilia, a mother in one of my classes, had been working on avoiding criticism with her son, Paul. As is so often the case, life offered her the perfect opportunity to really test her new approach. Paul came to her and said, "Mom, I have something to tell you, but I'm afraid you're going to get mad."

Cecilia gulped, but remembered not to jump to negative conclusions. "It can't be that terrible," she said calmly. "As long as you are safe, nothing can be that bad. Tell me."

"You know your new bike?" Paul said, cringing. "I borrowed it."

Cecilia realized that there must be more to Paul's confession, and allowed him time to muster up his courage. "I scratched the fender."

Cecilia took a deep breath. "I really like my bike," she said, "but we can repair the scratch."

Paul was visibly relieved. "Are you sure you're not mad at me? I'm really sorry."

"Paul, I'm upset that you borrowed my bike without asking me, but it's just a scratch. The most important thing was that

THE MAGIC OF ENCOURAGEMENT

you had the courage to tell me what you did. I really appreciate that." Cecilia told me later that this moment was a real turning point in her relationship with her son.

Cecilia could easily (and some would say justifiably) have exploded at Paul, but instead she used the opportunity to encourage his honesty. Far from indifferent, Paul's mother let him know that she was upset, but without attacking him personally.

It is especially hard to praise our children when they misbehave or when things go wrong. Although Cecilia's response may seem to you to be beyond the capacity of merely mortal parents, with practice you too can learn how to take even the most negative situation and focus on the positive.

It's all a matter of where we put our attention. Imagine that your friends had done the same thing. You probably would have said, "No problem. That's easy enough to fix." Isn't it strange that it's easier to be gentle with the feelings of people we care less about than with those people closest to our hearts?

Super Praise

One of the best ways to express your appreciation is through a technique developed by author Lee Canter, in his book *Assertive Discipline,* called Super Praise.[7] It is a powerful tool to reinforce your children's good behavior while boosting their self-esteem.

There are three steps to Super Praise:

First, praise your child. "I appreciate the way you did your homework without me reminding you." Be sure to direct your praise to the activity rather than to the child. "You're a good kid" doesn't carry as much information as "I like it when you pick up your toys after you and your friends finish playing."

Second, praise your child in front of another adult. "Billy did his homework today without me having to remind him."

"Sally picked up her toys after Jenny left."

Third, your partner or a friend also praises the child and gives him or her a hug.

"I really like getting such good reports from Mom about you. I bet you're proud of yourself."

This technique works best with younger children. Teenagers are too self-conscious for you to talk about them in front of other people. Get into the habit of praising your child at least three times a day. Helping children to feel good about themselves is the key to good behavior. Success builds most naturally and easily on past successes. Kids are most likely to believe they can be successful when they have a history of similar experiences.

Exercise: I saw someone doing his/her best: This is a structured activity to help you to focus on your children's efforts and accomplishments.

Make a poster entitled "I saw someone doing his/her best" and put it up in a visible place. Then, whenever you see someone doing a good job or trying his hardest, write it down on the poster along with his name. For example: "I saw Will feeding Leroy," or "I saw Anna working hard at her homework." This activity will support you in focusing on and commenting on your children's efforts. And it makes your praise for your child concrete. Kids can also write appreciations and accomplishments on the poster: "I saw Mom get up early and exercise today."

3. GIVE POSITIVE SUPPORT FOR EACH STEP IN THE LEARNING PROCESS

Don't wait until your children have accomplished a major task to encourage and support them. Imagine what would have happened if, when your child was learning how to walk, you said, "Look at you. You've already fallen down five times, you're never going to learn. You might as well give up now and go back to crawling. You keep making mistakes, you're hopeless."

Most of us ooh and ahh when our children pull themselves up and hang on to a chair. When they attempt their first step, we call the grandparents, send telegrams, and alert the media. We get really excited, and say things like, "That's it! Look how well you're doing! Keep it up. Atta boy." We don't wait until they can walk or run around the block to encourage them and support their new efforts. We can use this same approach with every area of our children's lives in which we want improvement. We can break the learning process down into smaller, more achievable goals so our kids can feel successful all along the way.

Notice their efforts and small achievements. For example, "I see all your toys in the basket. Do you want some help putting them in the closet?" "Putting the napkins on the table was a big help. I'll finish the job with the silverware."

Enter at Your Own Risk

We call my daughter's room "the pit." She has a sign on her door, BLESS THIS MESS. Periodically I ask her to clean her room. An hour later she'll be sitting at her desk arranging her makeup and pens, and organizing her papers. All around her is a disaster area. Clothes are everywhere. Magazines litter the floor. But her desk looks wonderful. I have a choice. I can say, "This place still looks like a hurricane hit it! At the rate you're going, it's going to take you till the year 2000 to get it cleaned up!" Or I can say, "Your desk looks great! You've made a good start. Keep up the good work." Don't you think she would feel encouraged and more likely to continue with the latter response? We have a choice of what to focus on in every situation. Remember: Positive motivates.

You Can Do It

I was at a preschool recently, and the teacher asked a group of three-year-olds to get ready to go inside. Rocky, a shy red-head, came up to her for help in taking off his jacket. Mary asked him if he needed help, and he said, "I can't get the zipper undone." She started the zipper, and he pulled it down the rest of the way. Then Rocky stood there waiting for her to do the rest for him. Mary encouraged him to do it himself. He struggled to get his arms out of the elastic sleeves. She said, "That's not easy to do, but you can do it. Keep pulling." He tugged at it and struggled, and finally it came flying off. Rocky ran to his cubby, shouting, "I did it, I did it all by my-self!" If Mary had taken Rocky's jacket off him, she would have robbed him of the experience of struggling, and there-fore of the success that the struggle produced. As a result of this seemingly insignificant experience, Rocky's self-esteem increased.

Our challenge as parents is to be patient enough to allow our children to take ten minutes to do something that would take us two seconds. We need to allow our children to develop what I call their "struggle muscle." This is developed the same way any other muscle develops, through regular exercise.

We can celebrate improvement and effort before our kids reach their final goal. When we focus on the small steps along the way, they get the message that "even if I don't get every-thing right, my parents still notice and appreciate what I do. It's worth making the effort."

4. SHOW CONFIDENCE

Supporting our children in learning new behaviors and mastering new skills is an avenue for building and sustaining self-confidence. Self-confidence is built through action and participation.

Confidence doesn't apply to the total child, but varies from one area of her life to another. Your child may be confident at school while unsure of himself in social situations. Or she may feel confident at playing tennis and lack confidence when it comes to academic matters. One of our goals is to help our kids to gain confidence in all areas of their lives. Kids who are self-confident are willing to take risks and accept challenges.

I was recently at the YWCA pool and overheard a mother screaming at her daughter, "Valerie, don't go near the pool, you can't swim. How many times have I told you that you'll drown if you go near the water!" It was a repeated harangue: "You don't know how to swim! Be careful! How many times do I have to remind you that you can't swim?" Of course, we have to watch our children carefully near water and be sure that there is sufficient supervision. But Valerie's mother was planting the seeds of self-doubt and fear in her child. She could have just as easily supported Valerie in becoming comfortable in the water by taking her into the pool and saying things like, "Swimming is wonderful. It's so relaxing and fun. Let's just splash around a little together and get used to being in the water." Confidence is gained by doing, taking action, and getting involved. The more your kids have exposure and experience in a new arena, the more they will become confident of themselves.

Expectations: The Self-Fulfilling Prophecy

In 1968 Harvard professors Rosenthal and Jacobsen created the Pygmalion experiment. They took a class of elementary school children and told their teachers that they had tested the kids and that certain of the children were gifted and had high IQs, and that the others were of average intelligence. In reality the researchers had used the students' locker numbers for their IQ scores. Rosenthal and Jacobsen were fascinated to find that the children who were labeled gifted did in fact excel in school, whether they actually had high IQs or not. They noticed that teachers gave the "gifted" students more opportunities and more time to answer questions, called them by name more often, and stepped closer to and touched them more frequently.[8]

Our kids rarely question our expectations of them; instead, they question their own sense of adequacy. When we have faith in our kids, they in turn grow to have faith in themselves.

Sometimes We Ask for Trouble

Many times, without realizing it, we expect the worst from our kids, thereby setting the stage for a self-fulfilling prophecy. When we talked about encouragement in one of my seminars, a mother, Kate, confessed that she was continually making negative comments to her daughter, Janice: "I'm warning you, no fighting with your brother in the restaurant or you'll be sorry!" "I can see it now, your toys will be left strewn all over the living room floor!" "I'll bet money that you won't get your report done in time." "I can always count on you to get in trouble when Dad and I go out for the evening." The saddest part of this story is that Kate's predictions about Janice usually were correct.

Switch to the Positive

The class suggested that Kate try switching to a positive approach in her dealings with Janice for two weeks. Kate agreed, and two weeks later she reported that she had been scrupulously careful to encourage cooperative behavior from her daughter with statements like, "I know you'll put your toys away when you've finished playing with them," "I like the way

THE MAGIC OF ENCOURAGEMENT

you're getting started on your report, I bet you'll have it done right on schedule," "I appreciate how cooperative and helpful you are when Dad and I go out," and "I know I'll get a good report from the baby-sitter."

"The change didn't happen overnight," said Kate excitedly. "But after a week I could see that Janice was really trying to cooperate. It's amazing!" She smiled. "It's like she *wants* to please me!"

If we treat our kids the way we would like them to be, there is a good probability that that is how they will develop. In a study of adults who are considered to be high achievers in their fields from science to athletics to the arts, a common theme emerged. While not all of these achievers were considered exceptional as children, they all had parents who supported and encouraged them to give their best and to pursue their dreams.[9]

Our beliefs about our children have an enormous impact on their self-concept and behavior. Believe in your kids. Expect them to cooperate and to excel, and they will fulfill your expectations.

Our Kids Need Our Support

My daughter started high school last year, which is a big adjustment for most kids. During the first month of school, out of the blue her best friend, Wendy, decided to hate her. I chalked it up to hormones. But when Wendy proceeded to turn the other girls against my daughter, Ama came home from school devastated. We had numerous discussions about the situation, but Ama still went about feeling miserable. I kept saying to her, "I know it's hard for you, but if you can learn to love yourself no matter what anyone says or does to you, you'll be way ahead of the game. Even I'm still learning that one."

Finally I told her to use a phrase that a friend of mine, Jack Canfield, taught me. "No matter what you say or do to me,

I'm still a worthwhile person." She agreed to try. While she was in the midst of having paper thrown at her or notes passed about her, she would say the phrase to herself. Gradually her depression began to lift. By my continual support and encouragement to make new friends, she worked through the situation, and eventually Wendy and the other kids stopped teasing her and started to include her again.

If we aren't there for our children, who will be? If they can't turn to us, they'll use something else to numb their pain. And that something else is likely to be drugs or alcohol.

The language of encouragement isn't taught in schools. It's foreign to most of us and takes time to learn. As parents, we can set an example of how to find the good in all people. Children who live in a positive environment learn to be positive about themselves and others, and eventually even about you.

Letter of Encouragement

Take a moment and recall a time when one of your parents said something encouraging to you. What did that parent say or do? How did you feel? After this difficult period my daughter went through at school, I was so pleased about how she handled herself that I decided to send her a card. It simply said, "Ama, I really feel good about the way you handled yourself and the situation with Wendy. I love you. You're very special to me. I'm glad you're my daughter. Love, Mom."

It may have taken me a total of ten minutes to do this, but it meant a great deal to her. Guess where she put my letter? In her special box where she keeps her good memories.

A Vote of Confidence

Donna and her family had planned a month-long trip to Germany. They had made arrangements to trade houses with a German family. When she and her husband, Nick, discussed the trip with their seventeen-year-old son, Cary, he was less than enthusiastic about going. After several lengthy discussions they decided that Cary could bring a friend if his friend's parents paid for the airfare.

After months of planning, Donna decided to ask Cary and Peter to be the tour guides for the first part of their trip. She gave the boys the assignment of planning a three-day expedition to Munich. "You're in charge of where we'll stay, how we get there, what activities and sights we'll see," Donna said with confidence. "The entire itinerary is in your hands." Nick added, "I'd like for the two of you to plan the trip within a certain budget and then present the information to your mother and me."

Several days later Cary and Peter arrived at the house with an armful of travel pamphlets and a couple of library books on Germany. The research had begun.

Cary's attitude about the trip had changed once he was included in the planning process. By giving Cary and his friend the responsibility for planning a portion of the trip, Cary's parents involved the boys in a way that communicated to them, "We have confidence in your abilities and trust you to make good decisions." When we ask our children's opinions, use them as resources, or call on their abilities and talents, we cast a vote of confidence in their direction.

Exercise: Strength Bombardment: This is an activity that can be done on a long car trip, at dinnertime, or during a family meeting.
Guidelines:
1. Each person gets a turn at being the focus person, which means he is the one who receives the strength bombardment. His job is to listen without saying anything while the other family members call out things they love, admire, respect, and appreciate about him.

2. It is helpful to use phrases starting with "I," such as: I admire, I appreciate, I like, I respect, I love, I celebrate. For example: "I love your sense of humor." "I appreciate your getting to bed on time." "I admire your artistic ability," etc.

3. Each person gets sixty seconds to be the center of attention and receive the positive messages.

4. The message should be said directly to the person instead of the others gossiping in front of them. Say directly to Tony, "I love your smile," instead of saying to your husband, "I love Tony's smile."

5. A word of caution: If there is a pause in the bombardment, remind your family members that they have a choice. They can either say, "See? I knew I was the slug of the universe, and no one has anything good to say about me!" Or they can say, "They must be thinking of how to say something more elegantly."

—adapted from *Self-Esteem in the Classroom* by Jack Canfield [10]

5. NURTURE SUCCESS

Nothing builds children's self-esteem like success. Our kids need to experience success in two areas: success in relationships (feeling lovable) and success in work (feeling capable and competent). It's our job to help them develop an "I can do it" attitude and experience their capabilities both at school and at home. Through encouragement we can teach our kids that success comes with *cans*, not with *cannots*.

Celebrate Mistakes

Keep in mind that children are in a process of experimentation and learning, and making mistakes is an essential part of the process. If your children fail at something, it doesn't mean that they are failures; it gives them information about what not to do in the future.

The fact that your child is willing to try something new indicates that she is already successful. If our kids don't feel the pressure to do things right the first time, they are more willing to accept a challenge, knowing that failure is a natural part of mastery.

There is a wonderful story about Thomas Edison that perfectly illustrates this point. Edison was working on inventing a storage battery. He had worked on twenty-five thousand different combinations, and he still hadn't successfully solved the problem. A newspaper reporter went out to interview him and asked, "How does it feel to be a world-famous inventor and to have failed twenty-five thousand times?" Edison looked at the reporter in surprise. "What are you talking about, 'failed!'" he said. "Today, I know twenty-five thousand ways *not* to make a battery. What do you know?"

Winston Churchill was also raised on encouragement. An interviewer once asked him, "Sir Winston, what in your school experience best prepared you to lead Britain out of her darkest hour?" After thinking for a moment, Churchill replied, "It was the two years I spent at the same level in high school." "Did you fail?" inquired the reporter. "No," responded Sir Winston. "I had two opportunities to get it right. What Britain needed was not brilliance, but perseverance when things were going badly." We need to support our children in seeing failure as an opportunity for discovery and developing their inner strength.

Practice Makes Excellence

Everyone who has achieved excellence has experienced failure. The difference between the people who succeed and those who give up is that the ones who succeed see failure as part of the process instead of viewing it as an obstacle. Success and confidence go together. There are the doers in life and there are the observers, the people who sit on the sidelines and play it safe by criticizing the players and never getting involved.

To succeed in life you have to participate. How are your children going to learn and grow if they are afraid of taking risks? Taking risks means not being afraid of failure. When your children fail, it's cause for celebration. Having failed means they had the confidence to take a risk to learn something new.

Becoming a Cheerleader

One day Ama came home from school and said she wanted to try out for the softball team. I was stunned, since, as I mentioned earlier, she had never before expressed an interest in sports. "Why the sudden interest?" I asked her. She said that all her friends had tried out and were on the team.

We borrowed two mitts, a bat, and a ball, and went down to the beach to practice. I started to pitch some balls to her, and she was missing pretty consistently. After about ten minutes of no hits she said, "I can't do this. I'm never going to get on the team—I'm just not athletic." I told her it takes time to get in the swing of things, and to be patient and keep making the effort. I pitched her several more balls, and she gradually started to hit them. We practiced the rest of the week. Guess where I spent my spring afternoons? Watching girls' softball.

What do you think would have happened if I had agreed with my daughter when she was feeling discouraged? What if I had said, "You know, you're right. You're really uncoordinated, and you're just not cut out to do sports. You might as well give up now and go back to doing your artwork"? She would have felt hopeless and would have given up. Our children need our external support and encouragement when they are learning new skills until they can internalize their own confidence and self-support.

Your expectations and belief that your kids *can do it* is crucial in nurturing their growing sense of themselves and their talents. Confidence comes from taking risks and not being afraid of failing or making mistakes. We need to communicate to our children that the goal is not to attain perfection (which none of us reaches anyway), but rather to strive for excellence. Excellence is achieved only through practice and correction and more practice. When our children are afraid to make mistakes in the course of practicing a new skill, they greatly inhibit the learning process. We need to cultivate an attitude of "I guess you made a mistake. What can you learn from it?"

Recall Past Experiences

We are in a wonderful position to nurture our children's self-esteem through recalling their past successes. Every child has a history of achievements that makes him unique and documents his present capabilities. Keep track of your children's progress in various areas and tell them often how much more skillful, responsible, understanding, and adventurous they are now than they were a month or a year ago. Because we are a treasure chest of their triumphs and noble deeds, we can remind them in a difficult moment of how far they've come and who they really are. This goes a long way in helping kids recognize and appreciate their developing capabilities.

John, eight, accused Chris, seven, of stealing his skateboard. After a knock-down, drag-out fight, Chris came running into the house, tears streaming. "John called me a dirty liar and a rotten no-good thief," Chris sobbed. "I gave him back his skateboard yesterday, and now he's mad at me 'cuz he thinks I kept it." His mother sat down next to him. "Chris, you must feel awful. All those hateful names John called you must really hurt your feelings. But it's not what someone calls you that's important. It's what you tell yourself about yourself that counts. If John said, 'You have green hair,' would that bother you?" Chris smiled a little through his tears. "No, Mom, of course not." "Do you really believe that you are a thief and a liar?" Barbara continued. "No," Chris responded, "but it hurt my feelings that *he* thinks that." "Well," Barbara replied, "I remember the time you borrowed some money from me to buy a new model plane. The next week when I offered to give you your allowance, you reminded me that you had already spent it. You could have easily gotten extra money but you were honest enough to remind me. That sounds like someone who is honest and trustworthy.

"And remember the time when Dad went out to the garage to use his saw and couldn't find it?" Barbara continued. "You brought it into the garage all rusty, and admitted that you borrowed it and left it up in your tree house. That took a lot of courage." Chris sighed with relief. "Yeah, you're right! I am pretty honest!" he exclaimed. "Mom, thanks for reminding me that I am an okay person."

When we recount experiences in which our kids exhibited positive qualities with appreciation and respect, we reaffirm their strengths and help them to know themselves more fully.

Here is an exercise you can do with your children when you find them putting themselves down. It's called "turn-around statements." It's a way to change an old belief about themselves that no longer is true. Ask your child to state the old belief, followed by the new one. "I used to believe———, but now I know———." For example: "I used to believe I was a slowpoke, but now I know I'm on time." "I used to believe I was stupid, but now I know I'm smart."

Andrew Carnegie became one of the wealthiest men in turn-of-the-century America. When he came to this country as a small boy from Scotland, he did a variety of odd jobs. Eventually he worked his way to becoming the largest steel manufacturer in the world. At one time he even had 43 millionaires working for him. (Remember, in those days $1 million was worth the equivalent of at least $20 million today.)

A reporter once asked Carnegie how he had managed to hire 43 millionaires. Carnegie responded that those men weren't millionaires when they started working with him, that they had become rich under his tutelage. "How did that occur?" the reporter wanted to know. "Men are developed the same way gold is mined," Carnegie replied. "When gold is mined, several tons of dirt have to be removed to get an ounce of gold; but one doesn't go into the mine looking for the dirt—one goes in looking for the gold." [11]

Carnegie's astute assessment flawlessly describes the way to bring out the best in anyone, and most particularly your children. Don't look for the flaws and imperfections. Look for the gold. The more good qualities you look for in your children, the more you will find.

Children learn what they live and live what they learn. I'm convinced that the only way to raise positive kids is for us to become more positive ourselves.

The "I Can" Can: Take a tin can and have your child decorate it. Then write the words "I can" on it. Whenever your child learns something new or masters a new skill, have her draw a picture or write a few lines about her achievement on a piece of paper that will fit into the can. Roll the paper up into a scroll, date it and tie a ribbon around it and put it into the can. After several months have your child take out the scrolls and share her progress with your family.

Exercise: Achievement Board: Children love to share their accomplishments. You can have a bulletin board in the kitchen or family room on which your children can each record their achievements. The achievements recorded can range from athletic to academic, artistic, social, or just helping around the house. Have a box of stickers and stars handy so they can make Certificates of Achievement to post on the board. When the board gets too full, then they can transfer their certificates into an album and use it as a record of their past accomplishments.

Exercise: Switch to the Positive: What you see is what you get. This exercise requires that you shift your way of thinking and perceiving. Many annoying characteristics and faults we see in ourselves and our family members are strengths either carried to an extreme or expressed inappropriately. For example: Is your child loud and obnoxious, or enthusiastic and excited? Yes, his enthusiasm may need some tempering and redirecting, but it is a valuable quality. Write down three characteristics for each of your family members that you find either irritating or annoying. Then, next to each one, reframe it in positive terms. Think about what would need to happen to help mold that trait into a more positive expression.

Example:

Trait or Quality	Positive Reframing	What can you do to help redirect or channel the quality?
1. Sassy	Spunky	Help them find appropriate ways of expressing their feelings.
2. Wild	Enthusiastic	Give them outlets for their energy, physical and artistic.

3. Lazy   Introspective   Validate their need for quiet time and give encouragement for being more motivated.

Chapter 5
HELPING CHILDREN WITH FEELINGS

"Giving people, young people, a loving philosophic base for understanding themselves in order to prepare them to be on solid emotional ground as adults in the MOST important thing we can do."

—Edgar Mitchell, *Apollo 14* astronaut

Most of us grew up with parents and other significant adults who denied the intensity or the very existence of our feelings. They would say, "You've no reason to be so upset," "It can't be that bad," or "You're making a mountain out of a molehill." For those of us who were raised in homes where emotions were considered to be the enemy and to be avoided at all cost, it is not surprising that feelings still are a mystery to us now that we ourselves have become parents.

Learning to respond empathically to our childrens' emotions is critical in helping kids to feel lovable and competent, the two components to high self-esteem. One of our goals as parents is to help children *know* how they feel, and to teach them appropriate ways of expressing those feelings. But what do we do if we aren't 100 percent comfortable with our own feelings? How, then, do we help our kids? That's what this and the following chapter are about. The rest of this chapter will act as a how-to manual to help you to learn about your child's world of feelings. And I think you'll find that, in doing so, you'll learn a lot more about your own.

YANKING THE RUG

The first step in helping our children learn about their feelings is simple: We need to listen to and accept their feelings.

This sounds great on paper, of course, but the trouble is that in practice parents often do the exact opposite. Instead we say things like, "There's nothing to be afraid of." "You're just overly tired." "You're just in a bad mood because you're hungry."

We say these things because we think we are being helpful. But in reality we have the opposite effect. These phrases, and others like them, actually belittle and deny what our children are feeling. And denial, if repeated often enough, has a couple of surefire consequences. First of all, it infuriates our kids. And worse, it teaches them not only that they cannot believe their feelings, but that somebody knows how they feel better than they do.

Children can't help what they feel. The world of feelings is new to them, and they are continually flooded with strong emotions of all kinds. By acknowledging and accepting kids' feelings, we help them explore and define their emotions in a way that strengthens their sense of personal validity and self-worth. When we deny their feelings, it inevitably backfires on us. Our kids feel misunderstood and discounted. The feelings they are struggling to express and understand, if denied, may then be repressed and resurface in some other, less healthy way.

Speaking the language of empathy is a learned skill that most of us were not taught in our own childhoods. It takes time, lots of patience, and practice, practice, practice to be able to acknowledge and accept our children's feelings. But the outcome is well worth our effort. To feel is to be real. What a wonderful gift we give our children when we teach them to accept and respect their emotions.

But how do we do it? The first step is to become a sounding board for our children. Rather than trying to "make it all better," find a word that identifies what they are feeling. It is hard to watch our children struggling or in pain. We want them to be happy all the time. So at times we try to relieve them of their sad or angry feelings when that's not what they need at all.

Here's an example of what happens when we deny our children's feelings: Jimmy brought home a painting he did at school. He threw it on the kitchen table, looked down, and walked away. His mother called after him, "Jimmy, what's this?"

J: "It's nothin'."

M: "What do you mean, it's nothing? It looks like a picture to me."

J: "I hate it. It's ugly."

M: "Don't be silly. This is a perfectly beautiful picture."

J: "No, it's not. I hate it, and I don't want to go to art anymore. It's dumb."

M: "Don't be ridiculous. Of course you're going to art. I don't know why you don't like this picture. It's very nice."

J: "I hate it. Throw it away."

M: "I will not! I love your artwork, and I look forward to seeing what you do at school."

J: "I hate it and I'm gonna tear it up. And you can't stop me!"

Jimmy's mother thought she was doing the right thing by trying to make her son feel better through praise and optimism. However, instead of feeling better, Jimmy felt more and more frustrated and defensive of his feelings. Why? Because he didn't feel heard or understood.

What would you do if your child came in with a sprained ankle? Simple. You would put ice on it, wrap it in an Ace bandage, give her a kiss, and allow time to heal it. For some reason we have more difficulty attending to our children's emotional hurts. It's perfectly natural to want to comfort our children and to rescue them from distress. But when we do this before allowing them to explore their feelings, they are given the message that what they are feeling is wrong or inconsequential. They think that we don't care about how they feel. Their frustration and upset then gets transferred from the original situation to us. Jimmy started out feeling frustrated with his artwork, and ended up angry at his mom.

What Jimmy's mother could have done was to listen to her son's underlying message and reflect back to him what she heard him say. "You seem disappointed with your artwork." Or, "Sounds like you don't like your painting." Or, "What I hear you saying is you're frustrated with your art class." Any of these phrases would have let Jimmy know that his mother understood how he felt and given him an opportunity to further express himself. We will discuss this technique in greater detail later in the chapter.

When our children are expressing emotions, our empathy helps them not only to feel understood, but to feel as if they have an ally who respects them. By acting as a sounding board for their emotions, we become the perfect mirror for them to see, hear, and understand what they are feeling.

In many cases our kids are so involved in their feelings that they can't identify them. What can we do? We can start by asking ourselves the question: "How would I feel if I were in this situation?" Take a moment now and recall a time when your child was feeling very upset. What caused him to feel so upset? Now, ask yourself, "How would I feel if this were happening to me? " and notice what answer pops into your mind.

BECOMING A FEELINGS DETECTIVE

There are a number of ways to acknowledge our children's feelings, but one of the easiest methods is by restating or rephrasing them. Here's an example:

Mom: "How was your day?"

Sally: "Terrible. I hate Susie and Karen."

M: "You sound angry!"

Sally: "I am angry. I hate their guts."

M: "Something must have happened to really upset you."

S: "It did. They ran off and left me to walk home all by my-self!"

M: "I bet you felt hurt and left out."

S: "I did. I'd like to punch them in the nose!"

M: "You're really annoyed with them, aren't you?"

S: "Yeah, I'd like to flush them down the toilet."

M: "Gee, you seem really angry with them."

A while later the parent overhears Sally talking on the phone with her friend, saying, "I really didn't like being left out today." With her parent's support and understanding, Sally found a way to express her feelings and to work things out constructively with her friends herself.

When your children are really upset, they need a place to vent their feelings—not a lecture. When we deny our children's feelings, the feelings don't go away. They get repressed and begin to fester inside. When feelings are bottled up, they grow stronger. They come out later as temper tantrums, hitting, or bad dreams. When we accept our children's feelings, we are letting them know that feelings are a normal and natural part of life. We also save ourselves the grief of having to deal with inappropriate behavior later on.

It's easy to forget these principles, however. When things go wrong, we often tend to do the opposite of what we know we should do. We tell our kids what's wrong with them or play devil's advocate.

I can't even count the number of times I found myself saying things to my own daughter like, "How can you be hungry? You just ate." "What do you mean you don't like that dress? It's a gorgeous dress! It looks great on you." I was continually discounting her reality. It took a long time before I realized that when I denied Ama's feelings I was telling her not to trust herself. It never occurred to me that I was in effect saying that

I knew better than she what she thought and felt. Then I began to put myself in Ama's place.

Take a moment and imagine yourself in each of the scenes below. Notice how you're feeling after each response.

Scene #1: You come home from a hectic day at work. A co-worker criticized you in front of your boss. You lashed back at him in anger and left the office feeling frustrated, humiliated, and ashamed. That evening over dinner you begin to tell your spouse about the situation.

Your Spouse's Response: "What did you do this time? You know how provocative you can be. Maybe you deserved it. You know how you get when you're angry."

Scene #2: You are rushing to finish up some last-minute errands before picking up your kids at school. You race around the parking structure frantically looking for a space. There's one. You decide to try to squeeze your spouse's brand-new car into the small spot. As you try to maneuver your way into the space, you hear the sound of metal on metal. You get out to find a huge scratch on the front door. You tell your best friend about what has happened.

Friend's Response: "Oh, you poor dear, I feel so terrible for you. The new car! What a shame! I hope he won't want a divorce."

Scene #3: It's getting late, and after a day filled with anticipation you realize that your spouse has forgotten your anniversary. You are talking to your mother and you mention your disappointment.

Mother's Response: "He must be under a lot of stress to have forgotten your anniversary. What's going on that's distracting him so? Is everything all right between the two of you? I'm your mother; you can tell me."

HELPING CHILDREN WITH FEELINGS

Scene #4: You've been waiting in the doctor's office for an hour when the nurse finally comes out and informs you that the doctor has been called to an emergency, and you won't be able to see her today. As you are getting into the elevator you run into a friend and tell her what's just happened.

Friend's Response: "Come on. You don't need to be so upset! Life's full of unexpected surprises, and you have to learn to take them more in your stride. Cheer up!"

Scene #5: You have just done a week's worth of grocery shopping. You unload your groceries onto the counter. The checker totals your bill and you reach for your money. It's not there! Your face turns red, and you ask the clerk to wait while you run out to your car to see if you have left your wallet there. The six people in line behind you groan. You rush back into the store and report that you don't have any money with you. A woman in line mutters, "What a birdbrain." The clerk looks at you with disgust, sighs, and says that you can come back later to pick up your groceries. You dash out of the line and yell, "I'll be back soon."

Friend's Response: "Gee, that sounds like a nightmare! You must have felt really frustrated and embarrassed."

How did you feel when you heard each response? Did you feel accepted and understood? Probably not until the last one. When our feelings are denied (as in responses 1 and 4) we feel angry, misunderstood, and discounted. At the same time, if the listener gives our feelings more weight or consequence than we are giving them (as in responses 2 and 3), it makes us feel even worse. Our children feel the same way. When we deny our children's feelings, they think that they themselves aren't important and that we don't care about them. Their self-esteem suffers.

When I'm upset I mostly want my feelings to be heard. I don't need criticism or advice, and the last thing I want is speculation on the philosophical and/or psychological implications of my emotions. All this will succeed in doing is to make me feel even more upset and misunderstood and I am likely to withdraw altogether.

Children need an empathic listener when they are upset, too. When we listen and acknowledge their feelings appropriately, they are able to move through their confusion and to solve their own problems. Really listening to our kids is the quickest way to help them help themselves.

By listening, we express our interest and caring. It is a powerful tool to enhance our relationship with our children and to increase their self-esteem.

We have trouble being empathic listeners, though, when our children are revealing powerful feelings we just wish they didn't have. Your son rejects your "stupid" advice and takes the after school job. Your daughter says that she hates visiting her aunt, and it's your favorite sister that she doesn't want to see. But putting the lid on a boiling pot isn't going to make it stop boiling. It just adds to the increasing pressure. I'll say it again: Feelings don't vanish through denial. They intensify.

NEGATIVE FEELINGS ARE A FACT OF LIFE

When children feel compelled to deny their feelings, it is often because they believe that they're bad or wrong to feel the way they do. Negative thoughts, such as "To please my parents I have to put on an act" or "If they only knew how I really felt, they'd stop loving me," cause what is called *inauthentic behavior*. Children who resort to inauthentic behavior unfortunately often lose touch with all their feelings. They become numbed to their own feelings of affection, love, excitement, and joy along with their sadness, fear, and rage. Over time they are likely to create a *false self*, an artificial personality which they hope that their parents will accept more rapidly than their warts-and-all *real* selves.

Feelings don't appear on demand, nor can they be dismissed when they emerge at inconvenient times. The first step on the road to greater self-esteem and overall family harmony is to accept your children's strong feelings. The second step is to help them to release these feelings in constructive ways. The benefits to you and your child are clear. Not only do you avoid the sulking, whining, and grudge-holding behavior that are so indicative of a child's repressed feelings (and so hard to live with!), but you also help your children to enjoy their pleasant feelings more.

Here are five common ways that we unwittingly discount our children's feelings. Notice which ones sound most familiar to you:

1. Denial: "How can you possibly be tired when you just had twelve hours' sleep?"
2. Comparison: "Bobby isn't afraid of the water. What's the problem?"
3. Instruction: "You can't mean you hate the baby. You really love her."
4. Ridicule: "What a wimp! Are you going to cry over a little scratch?"
5. Threats: "If you're going to whine just because you weren't picked for the starting team, maybe you shouldn't be on the team at all."
6. Sarcasm: "I just *love* hearing about how much you hate my cooking in front of your grandmother!"[1]

Most of us have used these responses in some form or another at various times. We think we are being helpful, but children find this kind of talk intrusive and demeaning. It leads them to doubt their ability to assess the world around them, and stunts their budding sense of self.

THE EQUALITY OF FEELINGS

Traditionally in our culture women were allowed to express feelings, while men were supposed to remain stoic in the face of sadness and pain. Males who expressed their hurt or sadness were labeled wimps or sissies. Boys and men were taught that expressing such vulnerable feelings was taboo, so they learned to hold them inside and to pretend they didn't exist. Anger, however, was reserved for males.

Times are changing. People are realizing the importance of expressing the entire range of emotions. Despite these changes, people still feel uncomfortable seeing a boy cry, or a girl get angry. It is essential for children, regardless of their gender, to have the opportunity to express all of their emotions.

Think of children as having emotional tanks. When they are full, they need to be emptied out before any new information or experiences can go in. The simple act of listening allows our children to empty out their feelings and concerns.

In one of my workshops a mother reported her son's response after she acknowledged his feelings. He said, "You've always been in my face and on my case. Now you're on my team."

ACKNOWLEDGMENT DOESN'T MEAN APPROVAL

Some of you might be thinking, "If I allow my child to express all her feelings, I'm condoning everything she does." This is a common misconception. The truth is we can accept our children's feelings without allowing unacceptable behavior.

Beth asked her mother, Laura, for an ice cream cone after school. Her mother didn't want her to eat ice cream so she said, "No." However, Laura could accept Beth's disappointment and anger at being told "no" without allowing her to have the ice cream. "I know you'd really like to have the ice cream," Laura said, "*and* we're not buying ice cream today." We can allow our kids to have their feelings while setting clear, firm boundaries on their behavior. Just because they have a desire doesn't mean that we must fulfill it, or that we're terrible parents for saying no. When we acknowledge our children's feelings it doesn't mean we agree with them. It simply means that we hear them.

Here are five basic and highly effective tools for acknowledging feelings:

- Listen attentively.
- Identify what they are feeling.
- Let them know you are listening by making reassuring sounds.
- Grant them their wishes in the realm of make-believe.
- Share your similar experiences and feelings.[2]

Let me elaborate.

Listen attentively. Listening attentively first means that you make eye contact with your children. Either sit on a chair or kneel down so that you are at equal eye level.

Second, take this time to clear your mind of any extraneous thoughts. Be with your child fully. Have you ever had the experience of talking to someone while he or she is reading the newspaper or watching television? It's very frustrating and annoying. Give your children the gift of your uninterrupted attention, which then allows them to explore their feelings more deeply. This will communicate your caring, concern, and genuine interest in them and what they are about to say.

Third, listen. Don't talk. Good listeners are in short supply and in high demand. When we jump right in with instant advice, we deprive them of discovering their own solutions through wrestling with their problems. In other instances we may feel uncomfortable with either the intensity or content of what they are saying, and we talk to alleviate our own discomfort. Neither approach supports your kids in expressing themselves.

Fourth, look into their eyes and touch them. The keys to making this process work are to give them your undivided attention, to be with them fully, and to listen to what they are saying.

There are times when it is not convenient or appropriate to stop and acknowledge your children's feelings. You may be busy with something else that can't be interrupted. Sometimes you're just too tired or preoccupied with your own thoughts to muster the energy to be a good listener. If you come home from a stressful day at work, you may need a few minutes' peace and quiet before tackling your kids' needs. If you walk in the door and see your children ready to devour you, give them a hug and say, "I know you want my attention, and I need fifteen minutes to cool out and collect my thoughts. Then I'll be ready to be with you." It's essential to take care of yourself so you can better take care of your kids. When we do this, our children grow to recognize that parents have needs too, and that we care enough about them not to pretend to listen when we have too much on our minds. It is better to be honest with them rather than to try to fake it.

Children are very sensitive, and will pick up on your distraction and interpret it as a lack of interest or sincerity. If the situation arises where your child wants to talk with you and you have something that needs your immediate attention, say to her, "I want to hear what you have to say, and right now we have to go. Let's talk when we get home." Listening actively requires your participation and commitment to understand and support your child. Your attention says, "I care about you. You are important to me, and I'm here to help."

Identify what they are feeling. There is no such thing as a "wrong feeling." There are unpleasant feelings and uncomfortable feelings, but feelings aren't right or wrong. When we acknowledge our children's feelings it doesn't mean we agree with them.

Feelings are simply messengers bringing us information about our children's needs.

Children have intense feelings and very little experience in communicating them. When kids are upset, they're so immersed in their feelings that often they can't identify them. At these times we can help them understand their underlying needs by giving their feelings a name. We need to help our kids identify what they feel even if they don't know why they are feeling it. Then they are better able to cope. Many times our children are unaware of their feelings. But when we label them, children immediately recognize the truth of the label.

For example, your son comes in from playing with his friends and says, "Joey's mother won't let him play." What is he feeling? Decode his message by first asking yourself "What is the feeling tone hidden in this statement?" Second, pay attention not only to his words but also to his body posture, his tone of voice, and the quality of eye contact. Is he happy and excited, or does he sound dejected and sad? Does his stance indicate anger or fear? Respond to the feelings you observe as well as the story you hear. Choose a word or words that describe his feelings. Become what psychologist Haim Ginott called an "emotional mirror" and reflect back to him what it is you think he's feeling.[3] "You seem disappointed that Joey can't come over to play." This reflective response may be an opening for your child to explore his feelings more deeply, to get them off his chest, and to think more constructively about what alternative plans he could make.

A preschool teacher came up to me the other day and said, "I feel like I'm playing God when I tell a child how she feels." I suggested that she use more tentative phrases such as "seems like" or "sounds like." This give the child room either to validate or to dispute your suggestion. For example, instead of saying, "You're sad," try "You seem sad, Robin." Rather than "You must be afraid of him," say, "Sounds like you're afraid of him."

There are exceptions to this rule. With older children you

can turn their statements into clarifying questions. Make sure, though, that the question shows your empathy. "Mrs. Jones never calls on me in class." You respond, "You mean she doesn't include you in the discussions?" Generally, older children will respond with more information and you'll discover what's really bothering them.

Here's a cautionary word: When acknowledging children's feelings, don't use their exact words. If we sound like a taped playback, they'll doubt our caring and willingness to listen. Sometimes all that's required is to use synonyms. Billy might say, "I hate Paul." You might reply, "You sound mad at him."

After having listened to a child's tale of woe, it is often effective to summarize what you've heard. You can use phrases such as "Let me see if I've understood this. You and Sally were on the swings and . . ." Or "Sounds like you were scared." Or "I'll bet you were frightened." If you've misunderstood, this will give them an opportunity to correct you. Summarization also helps to further clarify for both you and your child what they are feeling, and lets them know you've heard and understood every nuance of what they've said.

Acknowledge their feelings with reassuring sounds such as: "Uh-huh," "Yeah," "Oh," and "Mmm." While "silence is golden," it is not always the most effective invitation to encourage our children to share their feelings. When kids are upset, they need something more than just silent listening.

Our children need reassurance that we are truly interested in what they are saying. Trivial though it may sound, a simple "uh-huh" or "mmm" tells our kids that we are listening with our full attention. Expressing feelings isn't easy and kids need to know that it is safe to go on talking. Sometimes a mere "I see" is all they need. *Reassuring sounds* say, "I hear you, and I want you to continue." Active listening is not really complete silence. Active listening is punctuated with grunts of caring and understanding. These sounds tell our child that we are genuinely interested and that it's safe to share more.

Grant them their wishes in the realm of make-believe. One Monday morning when my daughter was six I was having a terrible time getting her up and dressed for school. Ama kept whining about how tired she was. Rather than getting frustrated I decided to handle it light-heartedly. I said, "Gee, Ama, I'm really tired too. Wouldn't it be great if the whole house were made of pillows? We could snuggle up and take a nap anytime we wanted to!" Then she chimed in, "Yeah, Mommy, and wouldn't it be fun if the yard was made of pillows and the street and my classroom, too!" We ended up giggling and playing our "The world is made of pillows" game as she got dressed.

By taking a potentially tense situation and making light of it, I avoided an angry confrontation. It is not always possible or even desirable to give your children what they want. But by having their wishes acknowledged, they at least feel as if someone understands them. Children are often willing to be distracted, and by using this technique, which was first pioneered by psychologist Hiam Ginott, both you and your kids can better cope.

Share your similar experiences and feelings. Sharing a story about yourself when you were in a similar situation is another effective tool for connecting with your children. For example: "I remember when I was invited to spend the night at my friend's house and at the last minute she called up and said she forgot and made other plans. I felt really angry and hurt." Your child will see two things: that she's not alone in her feelings because you struggled with similar issues; and that, like you, she can survive them. When you use this approach be careful not to become the focus of attention or to use the story to minimize your child's upset.

AVOIDING THE FIX-IT GAME

Another important thing to remember is that when our children tell us about an upsetting event or a relationship, they don't really want us to change the situation. What they need instead is for us to understand their feelings about the event or interaction. When our children are upset with their friends, a teacher or a situation, it is best to *respond to the feeling tone* rather than to the *content* of their words.

Here's an example of what happens when you play into the fix-it game. One day when my daughter was in sixth grade, we were driving along and she got this sad look on her face. She said, "I don't have any friends." I responded, "What do you mean, you don't have friends? Cathy and Chrissy are your friends."

A: "They go off together and leave me out."

M: "They were just at our house this afternoon. They weren't leaving you out then."

A: "Yeah, but one minute they act like they like me, and the next minute they're talking behind my back and making plans without me."

I was furious, feeling my daughter's pain and remembering my own pain at being left out. I said to her, "I'll call Cathy's mother and talk to her."

The next day after school Ama and her two friends came in laughing and carrying on like nothing had ever happened. I quickly realized that I needn't have called Cathy's mom. I had mistakenly listened to the content of Ama's complaint, i.e., "My friends are leaving me out," instead of listening to the feelings beneath her words. What Ama was really saying—and what she needed me to hear—was "I'm lonely. I feel insecure right now and I'm not sure how likable I am." She didn't need me to solve her dilemma for her no matter how easy it might be to fix. What she had wanted from me was empathic listening and acknowledgment of how bad she felt in the situation, not for me to get involved in her problems.

This is one of the hardest challenges in listening to our children—to keep from making suggestions, giving advice, or solving their dilemmas. As parents, we are conditioned to want to make it better. And sometimes we doubt that our child has the ability to cope with or solve the problem alone. However, try to remind yourself that the odds are that your child isn't so much desiring a solution as wanting to share the experience with you. Continue to accept his feelings and he will come to his own solutions. If you do need to step in you will have plenty of time later, after the feelings are handled. Just remember, when your child can create her own solution, it will do more for her self-esteem than having you solve it. Many times the solution becomes more obvious after she has had the time to express her upset, and is less angry or disappointed.

All parents want to protect their children from every potentially painful situation. Unfortunately, that's not within our power. But what we can do is to let them know that we hear them, that what they are feeling is okay, and that they are not alone. Time will do the rest.

The most important thing to remember is that it is our caring and compassion, not the particular words we use, that will make the difference with our kids. Children are like finely tuned radar receivers: They can sense the difference between a sincere, caring parent and one who is just going through the motions. If we are genuinely concerned, they'll know it and feel loved.

LOGIC VS. FEELINGS

Feelings aren't changed by using logic, reasoning, or presenting indisputable facts. It doesn't work on adults. And it never works on kids. Imposing logic on feelings is like trying to merge oil and water; they just don't mix no matter how hard you try. Here's a classic example from one of my seminars:

Clay, a five-year-old, lives with his mother, a single parent. Amanda often has to work on the weekends, and on these occasions, Clay stays with his grandparents. One Saturday just before Clay was about to be picked up, he said, "I can't go to Grandma and Grandpa's today. I have to stay and play with my friends." Amanda replied: "Don't be silly. Of course you're going. I have to work. Now come in here and get ready."

C: "Larry and Josh are building a tree house and I have to help."

A: "You love going to Grandma and Grandpa's. You know you have fun when you're there."

C: "I don't want to go. I want to play with my friends."

A (now getting really annoyed): "Clay, you can work on the tree house when you get back. Now get ready."

C (bursting into tears): "I really want to build a tree house."

Because Clay was trying to express his feelings and because Amanda was trying to use reason and logic to answer him, it was as if they were talking two different languages. No wonder Clay felt frustrated and misunderstood afterward. His mother had had a hard time acknowledging Clay's feelings because of her own guilty feelings. When Amanda talked about this in class, she was very upset because she felt guilty about having to ship her son off to her parents whenever she needed to work.

If Amanda had been able to empathize with her son's anxiety and ambivalence she could have said, "It's hard to have to live in two places. Sounds like you wish you didn't have to go back and forth between our house and your grandparents'."

Amanda didn't have to come up with a solution to the problem. All she had to do was to listen to her son's pain and to acknowledge it. The hard part is when our children's hurts press some of our own tender emotional spots. But in order to help them understand their feelings, we must differentiate their feelings from our own.

R-E-S-P-E-C-T—FIND OUT WHAT IT MEANS TO ME

There are times when your children just don't want to talk. No matter how interested or concerned you are, they just want some time alone to be with their feelings.

One mother reported that her teenage daughter came home from school crying. She said to her, "You seem really sad." Her daughter responded, "I am." Her mother continued to stand there and to wait for her daughter to say something more, but the girl walked into her bedroom. The mother said, "I'm interested, and whenever you want to talk, I'd like to hear what's bothering you." An hour later her daughter surfaced and told her about the fight she had had with her boyfriend.

It's important to respect your children's need for privacy while giving them an open invitation to talk when they are ready. This kind of respect is an investment in communication. At the times when your child does open up to you and shares his thoughts and feelings, it is important for you to listen attentively without making light of or judging those feelings or ideas. This will encourage him to talk with you more openly in the future about weightier matters. It's also important to let your children know that you are interested in their thoughts and ideas. Saying things like "How do you feel about . . . ?" or "I'd like to hear what you think about thus and so" are good openers.

MISBEHAVIOR REQUIRES IMMEDIATE ATTENTION

There are also times when simple, clear limits are called for rather than empathic listening. If your child is jumping on your bed, this is a time to say, "Jumping is for outside, not on my bed." Then take your child outside to jump on the mini-trampoline. It's not a time for you to be empathic and say, "I know you're sad because you couldn't jump on my bed." If your child is running across a busy street, it's a time to take action and to be very firm and clear with her where her safety is concerned. It's not time to say, "I bet you'd like to cross the street on your own." We need to say, "The street is very dangerous, and until I can trust that you know how to cross safely you'll have to play in the backyard." In these cases their feelings don't need your immediate attention, their *behavior* does.

DO AS I DO

We can also help our children become comfortable with their feelings by expressing our own: "I'm glad you've finished doing your chores, but I'm angry that I had to remind you so many times" or "I enjoy taking walks with you" or "I'm frustrated trying to figure out this computer program."

Children listen to and absorb feelings, not words. They don't learn from being told; they learn from watching and picking up what we do. Be a good role model in how you deal with your own feelings, and share some of your coping skills with your children.

A friend of mine thought that honesty was an important value to impart to her children. Karen said that one day the phone rang and she called to her daughter, "If it's for me, tell them I'm not here." Karen in that moment realized that she was modeling dishonesty for her daughter. She decided to take the phone call and then later spoke to her daughter about her decision. Karen has never asked her daughter to lie for her since.

Every day we are models for our children. How can we demand that they become loving, thoughtful, and responsible without modeling it for them? Our children learn through our interactions with them. We are teaching our kids all the time without knowing it. It's important to ask yourself, "What it is I want my children to learn?" Then *be* more of that. If you want your children to be loving, model loving behavior. If it's discipline, be more disciplined yourself. If you want them to learn to be more creative, express more of your own creativity—they'll pick it up by osmosis. You are the mentor to your children: They absorb you and how you relate to them and to the world. As we express our feelings to our children we let them know more of our humanness.

Learning how to respond empathically to our children's upsets is the first step in helping children to feel more self-reliant. What stops us too often from acknowledging their feelings is our own intense emotions. But our all-too-human responses should not discourage or dissuade us. What we all want are kids who can effectively cope with difficult situations and their feelings of disappointment, frustration, and anger.

Our words are very powerful. They can evoke hostility or happiness. Our responses can make the difference between a home filled with conflict or one filled with love and support.

We need to be sensitive to our children and take our cues from *them*. No one technique is going to work all of the time. When we express our feelings and share our ideas we show them that we trust and respect them. Almost magically they begin to respond in kind.

PERSEVERANCE PAYS OFF

Don't get discouraged if your child doesn't immediately react favorably to your newly learned skills. Some children wonder why you're talking to them in this strange new way. One teen said to a student of mine, "Who are you and what have you done with my real mother?"

Some children become suspicious when we begin to acknowledge their feelings. They wonder what we want from them. One father said he almost gave up on this technique following his son's reaction. The boy said, "I hate my baseball team, the coach picks on me." He responded, "Sounds like you had a hard time at practice today." The son did not have a clue what his father was trying to do and instantly became angry. "Stop making fun of me," he said, now nearly in tears. When you begin relating with your children differently, the results at first are often somewhat less than satisfying. But if you continue to acknowledge and reflect back their feelings, they'll become accustomed to it, realize your sincerity, and new avenues of communication will begin to open.

When you accept your children's feelings, they feel more respected and connected to you. No matter how painful the situation may be, knowing that someone understands makes it easier for them to bear the pain or hurt. As children have their feelings mirrored back to them, they become more aware of their emotional landscape, and are better able to cope with life's challenges. Letting our kids know that we know how they feel demonstrates our genuine love and concern.

One of our main goals in parenting is to raise compassionate, self-reliant human beings. To build your child's self-esteem it is essential for you to find time to listen, and to listen in a way that demonstrates your love and caring. When you listen fully, what you communicate is two things: "What you say matters to me" and, more importantly, "You matter to me."

Our children hold the promise of the future. We are the caretakers who will help them to realize their full humanity. The family is the first, most important classroom. What our children learn at home is the basis for how they relate in the world. If we want a world of peace and harmony, we have to relate to our children with a sense of cooperation and caring. If we want our children to be confident and capable, we have to provide them opportunities to test out their sense of competency. If we want our children to act responsibly we have to allow them to make decisions and to live with the consequences of their choices. If we want them to be loving and compassionate, we have to respond with love.

In the larger view of our lives, there is no more valuable use of our time and talents than to give the world the gift of a loving, compassionate, aware human being. Regrettably, the world rarely gives recognition for this challenging job. That's why you need to remind yourself on a daily basis that the time and effort you expend on raising your children really matters. It is important that you make a point of giving yourself a message of love and appreciation for the successful, caring parent that you already are.

The following exercises will help you and your family become fluent in the language of feelings.

Decoding the Real Feelings[4]

The five statements are comments children make using coded language to express their feelings. Fill in the chart using one of the words listed below which describes what the child might be feeling. Then use the word to write a statement which shows that you understand what they are feeling.

Feeling Words:

Disappointed	Lonely	Happy
Angry	Embarrassed	Dissatisfied
Sad	Discouraged	Scared
Excited	Satisfied	Confused

1. "I hate Sam. He always gets picked for the football starting lineup."
2. "I miss Grandma. I wish she didn't live so far away."
3. "Tony invited everybody but me to his birthday party!"
4. "The art teacher doesn't like my drawings. Oh, well, I didn't like art anyway."
5. "There's no way I'm going to the beach this summer. I look like Miss Piggy!"

Child's statement	*Feeling Word*	*Your statement*
1. ———————————		
———————————		
2. ———————————		
———————————		

3. ————————————————————————————

————————————————————————————

4. ————————————————————————————

————————————————————————————

5. ————————————————————————————

————————————————————————————

Exercises:

Guess What I'm Feeling Game[5]

Take a stack of 3" × 5" index cards and write feeling words on them. Then have each person in your family pick a card and pantomime the feeling while everyone tries to guess the feeling that's being acted out. Ask someone to explain when and why they've also felt that way.

Feelings Inventory

In my seminars I ask parents to play a game I call "The Family Mapping Game." The purpose of this exercise is to discover the ways in which your own parents' attitudes and behaviors were transmitted and adopted. As you become aware of these early learnings, you are freer to choose the attitudes and pattern that you want to continue in your own families. Take a few minutes and answer the following questions.

1. What feelings were okay to express in your family when you were growing up?
2. What feelings were taboo? Were there some feelings that were less comfortable than others?

3. Recall some of the things that were said to you when you were a child that denied your feelings. How did you feel when you heard these denials?
4. What feelings do you have difficulty accepting and expressing now?
5. What feelings do you have difficulty allowing your children to express?

The good news is that all behavior is learned, and once you discover your basic assumptions and expectations, you have the opportunity to add new information and skills to your present repertoire.

Chapter 6
ANGER IN THE FAMILY

"Nobody's family can hang out the sign NOTHING THE MATTER HERE."

—Chinese proverb

Anger is the emotion that is most often misused and confused in our society. It blocks the expression of all our other feelings. For many of us, anger is scary. It scares us if someone else gets mad, and it scares us even more if the anger is our own. When we discussed the subject of anger in one of my classes, one father blurted nervously to the group, "I'm afraid of my temper. I don't know what I might do if I really let myself get angry. I might hurt my kids."

That's our greatest fear. If we get really angry, we could say or do abusive things that would cause irreparable damage to our children that we would deeply regret for the rest of our lives. We're afraid that the beast within us will rush out, and we'll be overwhelmed with rage. We'll have a temporary lapse of sanity and become dangerous.

Before we had children, most of us never imagined the rage our kids could provoke in us. I remember watching in horror as a mother, screaming at the top of her lungs, yanked her young son out of a supermarket cart and dragged him by his arm, crying, out of the store. I said to myself, that woman is insane. She must be a child abuser. Poor kid! And I repledged myself to my vow of never treating *my* kid like that. And then I had my own child.

THE DEMON EMERGES

I was a committed pacifist. I had studied the teaching of Gandhi and protested nonviolently in civil-rights marches in Washington, sitting in front of police barricades, refusing to be provoked to violent action. One day, however, my friend Patty and I were taking my daughter, Ama, to Disneyland. Ama, a master at pushing my buttons, had irritated me beyond the point of no return, and I flew off the handle and grabbed her by the arm. Later, while we were standing in line waiting to get into Space Mountain, Patty looked down at Ama and said to me, "What are those red marks on her arm?" Horrified, I realized that in my rage I had squeezed her arm hard enough to leave marks. Feeling too embarrassed to tell my friend the truth, I said nothing. But inside I was dying. How could I have so easily lost control and lashed out at my own daughter? I realized how easy it was to lose my temper with my child where in other situations I could remain calm.

We rarely talk about how angry our kids can make us. Our guilt feelings about the temper tantrums we throw shame us into silence. Secretly we feel that there is something wrong with us because we fly into uncontrolled frenzies. Yet in my seminars parents are relieved when I confess to my own fits of rage. They talk about their own intense feelings toward their kids, and admit that they consider anger immoral and abnormal. Yet the inescapable fact is that anger is a perfectly natural human emotion. Because our anger is directed at the people who are closest to our hearts, it is one of the most painful, frightening, and difficult issues we wrestle with as parents.

In this chapter you will learn how you can choose to express these primitive feelings in more humane, civilized ways. Learning how to express our powerful emotions constructively takes real effort and is an ongoing process. Fortunately it gets easier with practice!

EXPERTS AT PUSHING OUR BUTTONS

Four-year-old Jane refuses to leave her friend's house when her mother comes to pick her up. After much coaxing and a struggle, Jane's mother presses her to thank her friend's mother for having her over to play. Jane flies into a rage and runs out of the room shouting, "I don't like you! You can't make me talk!"

Eight-year-old George is sitting at the dinner table tapping his fork against his mug. His mother growls at him, "Stop that before you break it." George whines, "Lemme alone." He taps more vigorously until he knocks the mug off the table, sending ceramic shards and milk all over the floor. Joanne screams, "I told you! You break everything in sight. You never listen." George shrieks back, "You're a nerd! You never do anything right, either! You turn my underwear pink!" Joanne gets angrier until finally she drags George into his room and gives him a spanking.

WHY WE GET ANGRY

How do these little incidents—a broken glass or a few angry words—turn into major battles? What makes children say to their parents "I hate you. You're mean!"? What makes parents take comments like these as personal attacks or as acts of defiance?

Our children's anger arises from their feelings of helplessness at having so little control over their lives, or from feelings of being mistreated or misunderstood. Anger is a signal that one of their basic needs is going unmet or that their wishes are being frustrated.

These same things make us angry, too. When our kids refuse to cooperate, demand our undivided attention, throw temper tantrums, or strike out at us, we quite naturally get furious. We often say things we immediately regret, such as "Why can't you be more like your sister?" or "Even pigs don't live like this!" or "Great. Leaving your homework to the last minute was a really brilliant move."

We fall into what I call the "killer statement" syndrome: "You're a slob." "You're stupid." "You're good for nothing." "You're lazy." Our anger may be temporarily relieved, but at too high a price. Our children feel attacked and ridiculed by someone whose love, respect, and support they need desperately. They take our negative statements to heart and incorporate them into their self-images. Killer statements are not only harmful, but also ineffective. "You're a klutz!" doesn't provide any useful information about what they did that was upsetting to us, or what we want them to do differently next time.

It's as natural for children to feel angry and resentful occasionally as it is for us to feel frustrated with them. Still, it's very upsetting to hear our children express negative feelings, ones we wish they didn't have (especially loudly and in public). If we teach our kids to feel guilty about expressing their stronger, less socially acceptable feelings, they will repress them. If left unexpressed, they often resurface as depression, anxiety, or rebellion.

NO ANGER ALLOWED

Most of us were taught that anger was bad and to feel angry was to *be* bad. We were then encouraged to feel guilt for our anger, and were punished for expressing it. Consequently, most of us are ashamed and afraid of being angry, and at best try to ignore it or to deny that we feel it at all. In fact, there is an unwritten law that parents should never get angry at their children.

Emotions, however, are a part of being human. In order for our children to grow up feeling lovable and capable—the two components of high self-esteem—they need to know that their emotions are an acceptable, vital part of their personal experience. Moreover, they need to learn how to express their anger in ways that are appropriate and constructive.

Children are often afraid of their own strong feelings. At times they are overwhelmed with anger, sadness, or frustration. If on top of their fear about the feelings themselves, they feel your disapproval, then they will tend to repress these feelings or to cover them up. Any feelings that threaten their ability to give or receive love are good candidates for repression and denial. And, of course, the feelings we personally have difficulty expressing are the ones we tend to deny in our kids.

HOW TO HELP AN ANGRY CHILD

Let's make one thing clear at the outset: The children of "good" parents get angry, too. It's absolutely unavoidable, and is in fact a sign that your kids are developing a strong sense of self and self-will. That aside, there are several things you can do when your kids get angry that will help them express their feelings constructively.

WHAT DO YOU DO WHEN YOU'RE UPSET TOO?

First and foremost we must learn how to respond empathically to our children's upset feelings. Our empathic response will help them become familiar with the full range of human emotions, and will support them in feeling more emotionally competent and whole. The tricky part is to disentangle our own emotions about their upsets, so that we can clearly see and reflect back their feelings.

Whenever my daughter, Ama, came running into the house crying and hurt, my immediate reaction was anger. "Why can't you be more careful? If you didn't play such rough games this never would have happened!" It took me a while to understand my reaction. Finally I realized that I got scared when she hurt herself, and anger was my way of coping with fear. The last thing Ama needed when she got hurt was a mother who yelled at her. Once I understood my own emotions, I was able to respond more appropriately to the situation and to her needs.

Responding empathetically, however, does not mean giving in to our children's every whim. We can set firm behavioral limits while acknowledging the legitimacy of our kids' feelings. For example, "Sarah, I know you don't like it when I ask you to turn off the T.V., and it's time to turn it off now." "I know you feel frustrated, Robert, because you'd rather be at the park. But we need to go grocery shopping first." We have to be willing to withstand temporary rages for the long-term rewards of having children who grow up understanding reasonable limits and age-appropriate behavior.

GETTING PHYSICAL

Getting physical is another important approach to add to your bag of tricks. When children are very upset, physical activity is often the only effective outlet for their feelings. Encourage your kids to pound on pillows, throw balls at the garden wall, tear up newspapers, stamp their feet, or roar like a lion to let off steam.

When Maura's three-year-old son threw a temper tantrum, remembering one of the suggestions I'd given in our last class, she got down on the floor and said, "You sound like a really angry dinosaur. Can I hear how an angry dinosaur roars?" Then she let out a growl of her own to get him started. Billy caught the spirit and began roaring ferociously. Maura commented, "Wow, that sounds like a really angry dinosaur. Can you roar even louder?" Billy threw his arms up in the air and let out an even bigger roar. At the next class Maura reported that Billy had gone from raging on the floor to playing momma and dinosaur within a matter of minutes.

Another valuable and effective tool to defuse an angry child is to have them draw out their angry feelings on large sheets of newsprint. Although drawing or acting out feelings may not always be appropriate solutions, they are good tools for you to keep in mind with an extremely angry child.

For a lot of children, hitting is a spontaneous reaction to angry feelings. Jim's three-year-old son, Greg, would run up behind him and strike him on the legs. Jim, another parent in one of my classes, was shocked and uncertain about how to handle the situation. He asked for suggestions from other parents in the class. One recommendation was that he tell Greg, "It's all right to feel angry, but I don't like to be hit." Others suggested that he help Greg put his anger into words while clearly stating the house rules: "You're mad and I want to hear what you're angry about, but people aren't for hitting. If you want to hit, you can hit the pillow and yell 'I'm mad!' Pillows are for hitting, not people." Or, "I can see you're angry. Tell me with words rather than by hitting."

The technique Jim was counseled to use with Greg is called a "policy statement." Just as countries or companies have certain rules under which they operate, families construct their own set of behavioral rules. When your child violates these explicit rules, it's more effective if you state your objection to their behavior as neutrally as possible: "You have the right to feel angry, but in our house we don't scream at people, we scream into pillows."

If it's name-calling that bothers you, say, "When you're angry with me, tell me without calling me names. I don't call you names, and I don't like it when you do that to me." Policy statements acknowledge your child's feelings while reiterating the acceptable ways you'd like all family members to express themselves.

USE YOUR TEMPER—DON'T LOSE IT

Have you ever tried to be more patient than you felt? Anger is natural, and yet, because we often try to be calm and reasonable with our children despite our anger, what usually happens is that, down the road, Mount Vesuvius erupts. We're afraid our anger will be harmful to our kids so we hold it in. But holding in anger is like holding your breath. We can only hold it for so long, and then the inevitable happens. We have to let our anger out, and by that time it is usually way out of proportion to the situation. We can only be as generous as we feel. We can't fool ourselves into acting more patient or giving than we are. When we do this, resentment creeps in and then seeps out—or explodes—later.

A client of mine told me this story, which perfectly illustrates the problem: One evening Meg was sitting in her study doing some extra work she had brought home from the office. Her twelve-year-old stepson brought a friend home, and they went into his room to listen to his favorite tunes. The music was so loud that it made the walls of Meg's study vibrate. Meg did her best to concentrate on her work and ignore the music, thinking, "Oh, well, he's having a good time," until she finally realized that she had been staring at the same sentence for ten minutes. That was it. No more Patient Mom. Now, mad as an entire nest of hornets, Meg burst into her stepson's room and screamed, "Turn off that dreadful music!" Her stepson looked at her in amazement.

As parents we can learn to use our anger in constructive ways to solve problems in their early stages. Anger in itself is not bad. It's how we deliver it that causes it to be either a putdown or a lesson for our kids. One of the best tools in dealing with our anger is being aware of what I call "yellow alerts." A yellow alert is that first warning feeling in the pit of the stomach that tells you something is wrong. Most of us tend to ignore these signals, thinking that the problem will go away or that it's not worth our attention.

When we try to ignore the small warning signals, three things can happen: 1) The problem might actually disappear on its own (unlikely); 2) our anger will fester inside us and come out later in the form of sarcasm, withdrawal of affection, or in seemingly unrelated physical problems, such as headaches or an upset stomach; or 3) our anger will mushroom into a full-scale "red alert." We move into battle readiness and scream, shout, strike out, or react in some other habitual, unthinking, and destructive way. Pay attention to your "yellow alerts." Use them to choose a conscious path of action to handle a minor problem before it escalates into a major battle.

Our expression of angry feelings should give us some relief as well as offer our kids some insight into the effect their behavior has on us. The point of expressing our anger is not to make our children feel bad, but to make our feelings clear. Many parents think that they have to make their children suffer in order to get them to change their behavior. This just isn't true!

The reality is that the key to changing your children's behavior is to change how you interact with them. Trying to change *them* is like trying to swim against the current: It takes tremendous effort and usually doesn't work. It's much easier to change your own response.

When children feel defensive they have one of two reactions: Either they fight back, or they withdraw into their shells. When you shout, "You're an idiot!" your kids' automatic response may be adamant denial. Over time, however, they will start to believe what you tell them and to think of themselves as idiotic, sloppy, stupid, or disgusting. With a steady diet of "killer statements," your children lose their motivation to take risks and to try new things. Their strategy will become the avoidance of any further ridicule or criticism by playing it safe. They will shy away from competition or challenges and live under the motto, "If I don't play, I can't lose."

COPING STRATEGIES

One method to help you avoid dumping your angry feelings on your children is to breathe deeply and then count to ten. Sounds simplistic, but it works. If you reach ten and still feel agitated, *leave the room*. You are not obligated to stay engaged. Hitting your child or yelling hurtful things at her only teaches her that hitting or yelling is the thing to do when she gets angry. It is better to call "time out" rather than to model negative ways of coping with anger. Tell her, "I'm really angry right now. I'll talk to you about this when I calm down."

A second method for expressing anger constructively is a technique called "owning your feelings,"[1] made popular by Dr. Thomas Gordon in his book *Parent Effectiveness Training*. An effective formula is: "When you _____, I feel _____. What I want is _____." Here are some examples: "When I see your wet towels on the floor, I feel furious because it tells me that you think I'm your maid. What I want is for you to hang the towels up." "When you don't do your homework until the last minute, I feel concerned. What I want is for you to plan your time better." When we own our feelings, we can even express strong emotions without damaging our children's self-esteem. "I hate it when you leave your toys all over the living room floor!" Or, "I resent it when you tell me you'll come straight home after school and you show up late."

Many times our clear, nonblaming expression of anger will stop our children from acting out. Owning our feelings also teaches our kids that anger is a normal and natural part of life, and that it can be expressed in healthy, constructive ways.

OWNING YOUR FEELINGS

This exercise is to give you some practice in creating "I" statements using the formula suggested below. "I" messages communicate clearly how you feel about a specific situation, without blame, while letting your child know what you want.

1. Mary Jo is continually leaving the lights on when she leaves the room. Her father has asked her repeatedly to turn the lights out when she leaves the room.

   When you_____

   I feel_____

   What I want is_____

2. Craig has friends over after school. They hang out in his room and blast his stereo. His mother has asked him to play it at a more reasonable level, and he persists at keeping the volume loud.

   When you_____

   I feel_____

   What I want is_____

3. Jeffrey is responsible for walking and feeding the dog. His father has reminded him numerous times about his responsibility. Spuds, once again, is sitting by the door with a desperate look on his face.

   When you_____

   I feel_____

   What I want is_____

4. Carolyn uses the last piece of toilet paper on the roll and doesn't replace it with a fresh one. Her mother has hounded her about remembering to put a new roll out.

   When you_____

I feel———————————————————————

What I want is———————————————————————

ON COURSE/OFF COURSE

When it feels as if our kids are driving us crazy, it's easy to lose sight of our goal: to shape their behavior, to model the healthy expression of anger, and to do so without causing lasting harm. When we are in the heat of a battle, we often find ourselves wanting to make them pay for their wrongdoing, or wanting to get even for the misery and humiliation we feel. But if we can hold off from taking revenge, we will be a long way toward realizing this larger goal.

Remember those times when you *did* say the cutting words or hit your child. What feelings did you have afterward? My bet is that they were feelings of regret rather than relief.

As our children are exploring and experimenting, they need us to give them feedback to help them to stay on course. When the *Apollo* spacecraft carried the astronauts to the moon, it was off course much of the time and yet it reached its goal of putting the first man on the moon. The key to the mission's success was that the flight was constantly monitored. Whenever it strayed off course, it was given feedback to get it back on track. The feedback didn't say whether the craft was in a good or bad place. It simply told the astronauts where they were, and if there was a discrepancy, it let them know exactly what they needed to do to correct their course. The spacecraft was never allowed to go too far astray. Major problems were avoided because they were corrected when they were still small and manageable.

Frequently when we are telling our children that we don't like what they've done, our correction inadvertently takes the form of insulting, threatening, attacking, or rejecting. When correcting our children's behavior, it is especially important to be careful with our use of language and our tone of voice. Our tone can make the difference between the words being warmly received or defensively rejected.

Guess what percentage of our communication is done with our words? Researcher Albert Mehrabian reports the following breakdown; 7 percent through words, 38 percent through tone of voice, and 55 percent through our body language. Whew! That's something to think about.[2]

MISTAKES ARE FOR LEARNING

Patricia, a graduate of one of my seminars, told us that she had gone into her son Mark's room one day and was not pleased to see a recent addition to his decor—a large drawing of a marijuana plant that he had drawn himself. Upset, she asked him to take it down: "I don't want that kind of picture in my house." "It's my room," he shot back, "and I can do whatever I want in here!"

Patricia left feeling angry and frustrated. When she asked him to take out the garbage later on that evening, he resisted, delayed, and generally gave her a bad time. This sent Patricia into a rage. She stormed into Mark's room and ripped the poster off the wall. Several minutes later, she realized that she had made a mistake.

Remembering what she had learned in class, Patricia swallowed her pride, and went back into Mark's room and apologized. She said, "When I saw that poster on your wall, I got scared. I worried that you were either using drugs or interested in using them. I feel very strongly about your not getting involved in such destructive activities, but I had no right to destroy your artwork. I'm sorry." Patricia's apology reopened the lines of communication that are so vital to healthy relationships between teenagers and their parents.

When Patricia saw the drawing on her son's wall she immediately assumed that he was guilty of using drugs and convicted him on circumstantial evidence. It is too easy in these types of charged situations to react out of anger and create roadblocks to further communication. When we are faced with difficult and important issues, it is essential to keep the doors of communication open. But this won't happen if we simply react in anger. We must also share our concerns, deeper feelings, and values about such potentially self-destructive behavior with our kids. When we do this, they are more likely to respond honestly and openly.

None of us is perfect. Occasionally we are going to lose our cool and explode at our kids. When this happens, we should do what we would do were it a friend instead of just our child—apologize. We don't ever have to apologize for our feelings, just for how we behave. Apologizing for our own inappropriate behavior gives our children an opportunity to forgive and to experience more of our humanness. It also gives them a model for how we would like them to act in similar situations.

PARENTS HAVE FEELINGS, TOO

Soon after we explode at our children, we feel guilty. "What's wrong with me? How could I have such hateful thoughts about my child?" Carol recently told me that she got so angry at her four-year-old daughter that she wanted to leave her at preschool. Gordon confessed that he was so frustrated with his adolescent son's leaving his clothes in the hallway that he had fantasies of throwing them out the window onto the lawn.

Anger is a messenger who brings us valuable information about our needs. If we never express anger, our children may take it as indifference or lack of caring. They may also begin to believe that anger is wrong and must be denied or suppressed. Honest communication of our feelings is a gift to our children. It is not something to feel guilty about.

When I work with single parents, parents who are divorced or separated, or stepparents, the already-difficult issues of expressing anger and setting limits become even more complex due to the "special guilt factor." Regrets about denying their children a *Father Knows Best* childhood interfere with their ability to discipline effectively or to express their feelings.

Judith, for example, was concerned about the abusive language her sixteen-year-old son used with her. Josh would walk into the kitchen and say, "Not that crap again! You call that dinner? That shit looks like dog food. I'm not eating that." When I asked Judith how she felt when Josh spoke to her like that, tears flooded her eyes. "Angry and hurt," she said. Well, I continued, did she let him know the impact his words had on her? Her answer was immediate. "No, never."

This pattern is extremely common when parents feel as if they have to compensate for the lack of a second adult in the house, or the fact that their family is in a nontraditional form. They accept behavior from their kids which they would never accept from anyone else.

When you accept abusive treatment from your children, they learn that they have a license to misbehave because they have had some hard knocks. They will expect others to make exceptions for them throughout their lives. These same children will be in for an unpleasant shock when they learn that other people won't tolerate their foul language, rudeness, or inappropriate behavior.

ANGER DOES HAVE A PLACE IN PARENTING

Belle, a teacher, was visiting five-year-old Philip's family when he took a soccer ball and heaved it at his mother. The ball hit Daniella squarely in the stomach, and tears welled up in her eyes. Belle was genuinely concerned. "That looked like it hurt," she said. "Are you all right?" Daniella assured Belle that she was fine, and then smiled at her son.

What do you think Philip learned? He learned that it's okay to hurt his mother, that she doesn't mind when he acts rough. By denying her feelings, Daniella was teaching Philip that anger wasn't an acceptable feeling and that it needed to be hidden.

When we express our anger to our children in a healthy way, we teach them that we have feelings and that there is a limit to what we will tolerate. We don't need to explode all over our kids to communicate angry feelings, but they do need to know how we feel. The opposite of love isn't anger. It's indifference. Don't be ashamed of your feelings of anger and frustration. They are a sign of the depth of your caring. When you own your own anger and express it congruently rather than dumping it on your kids, it serves to inform rather than damage.

If Your Child Threatens to Run Away

It is important not to answer children sarcastically. Comments such as, "Let me help you pack," or "Who cares if you leave?" only compound the problem. Threatening to leave is our kids' trump card: It's their exaggerated effort to express pent-up anger and frustration. Don't take their threats as a personal attack or a slight against your parenting. They don't really want to run away. They just want to register their dissatisfaction with "management" in a way that will get your attention.

The Love Letter

When they are facing a problem in a relationship, most people tend to get stuck in one emotion—anger, fear, sadness—that painfully limits their ability to feel the whole of their emotional spectrum. The Love Letter is a sequenced writing activity developed by Dr. John Gray and Dr. Barbara De Angelis to help people to release the emotions that block the expression of their love.[3] This powerful tool can assist us and our older children in healing emotional upset when spoken communication is either physically impossible or counterproductive.

The Love Letter is an exercise of eight parts of roughly equal length:

1. Write down feelings of anger, resentment, and blame, using phrases such as: "I hate it when . . . I resent you for . . . I don't like it when . . . I'm tired of . . . I'm really angry that . . ."
2. Move to feelings of hurt and sadness: "I feel sad when . . . I feel hurt because . . ."
3. Next write about fears and insecurities: "I'm afraid that . . . I feel scared that . . . I'm worried that . . ."
4. Beneath the fears are usually feelings of guilt and/or regret for our part in the situation: "I'm sorry that . . . I didn't mean to . . ."
5. Under these feelings are unfulfilled needs or wants: "What I really wanted was . . . I want to . . . All I ever wanted was . . ."
6. Underneath the unexpressed desires is forgiveness: "I forgive you for . . ."
7. Then comes the appreciation: "I appreciate you for . . . I thank you for . . ."
8. And finally the love and caring: "I love it when you . . . I love you because . . ."

I've seen love letters heal rifts between teens and their parents, kids and their friends, older children and their teachers, employees and their bosses, adult children and their parents, and also between husbands and wives. The really magical part is that the letter doesn't have to be sent in order for it to work.

Exercise:

Anger Inventory

1. What is an area of chronic conflict you have with your child or children?
2. What about the situation makes you angry?
3. Is your anger helping you or hurting you in this situation?
4. What specifically do you want to change about the situation?
5. What do you usually do when you feel angry?
6. What are three alternative coping strategies you can use next time you feel angry?
7. When is your anger valid and justified?

By clarifying what we think, feel, and want, we can learn to use our anger in more constructive ways. It's amazing how quickly we are ready to enter combat without knowing what the war is about. Our most powerful position in implementing change is to begin to observe our patterns and discover new options for changing our behavior.

That Makes Me Mad

1. Have a discussion with your family in which all members tell five things that make them angry.
2. Then ask each other to explain why these things make you all mad.
3. List three things you can do to help your children positively channel their anger.

_____

_____

_____

Chapter 7
RAISING RESPONSIBLE KIDS

"Give a person a fish and you feed him for a day. Teach him to fish and you feed him for a lifetime."
—Chinese proverb

Ever since Tommy was a young child, he had a difficult time waking up in the morning and getting ready for school. His father would go into his room, turn on some soothing music, and gently say to his son, "Tommy, time to get up. Get a move on it, or you'll be late for school." Then he would go about his morning business. After several more calls Rick would gently coax his son out of bed and walk him into the bathroom. He would then escort him back to his room to help him get dressed. Day after day this early morning wake-up service continued. Tommy would drag himself through the morning routine kicking, complaining, and spreading a blanket of gloom throughout the household. Now, Tommy is thirteen and still receives the same royal treatment from his parents. Both they and he are convinced that if they alter the morning ritual, their son will be late for school.

Doesn't it sound like Tommy has wonderful, caring, nurturing, involved parents? They continually take the time to provide this early morning wake-up service to make sure that their son gets to school on time. Isn't he fortunate to have parents who are so dedicated and devoted—or is he, really?

Let's take a moment and evaluate this situation a little more closely.

WHAT IS RESPONSIBILITY?

Although Tommy's parents think of themselves as good parents, they are actually robbing their son of a valuable lesson. Through their well-intentioned help they are preventing him from acquiring the essential quality of responsibility. We all want to raise our children to be responsible human beings. But sometimes this lofty ideal seems easier said than done.

First of all, let's define the word itself. Responsibility is the ability to: 1) make choices and accept the consequences of your decisions, 2) recognize and accept limits, and 3) understand how cause-and-effect thinking works in the world.

We can't avoid making choices. Our lives are filled with decisions, from what clothes we are going to wear, to what time we will leave for work, to what we will have for dinner. Making choices is a fact of life. However, each choice we make has consequences—some small, some large.

What Rick and his wife, Ellen, are doing is protecting Tommy from experiencing the consequences of his actions. Under the circumstances there is no incentive for Tommy to make any effort to change his behavior and become more responsible. Why should he trouble himself to make changes when his parents perfectly anticipate and cater to his needs and requirements?

In teaching our children to become responsible, our primary attitude needs to be that each person is responsible for his actions and the resulting consequences.

Tommy had no idea that he was responsible for getting himself up in the morning. His parents weren't teaching him the connection between his actions and the results of these actions.

As I've mentioned earlier, there are two ingredients essential to your children's self-esteem: The first is for them to feel loved, valued, and accepted for who they are. Second, they need to feel capable, but they won't feel capable unless they are expected to handle responsibilities.

Once in a moment of complete frustration I turned to my daughter and screamed, "I'm not your slave!" I remember how she looked at me in utter shock and amazement, because she genuinely did not have a clue as to why I was so upset with her. After all, I'd catered to her for years, so what was my problem now?

When Rick and Ellen came to my seminar, Ellen was absolutely at her wit's end. "I'm tired of walking on eggshells around Tommy to make sure that he gets off to a calm beginning," she said when I asked her to describe the problem. "I feel like we are living with an emperor, and we are his servants! I resent his grumpy attitude and lack of cooperation. And I hate it that his bad mood dominates our house every morning!"

Her husband began to defend his son until his wife interrupted him. "Wait a minute, Rick. Hank and Ruth called me yesterday and asked us not to let Tommy spend the night at their house anymore. They said that he was too demanding, and it was unpleasant to be around him." Rick was dumbstruck for several moments. "I guess," he said finally, "it's time to make a change."

I suggested that they sit down with Tommy and discuss the morning situation, their concerns, and their new strategy. I told them to let him know that they felt it was time that he assume responsibility for getting himself up in the morning and ready for school. I then recommended that Rick take Tommy to the store to pick out an alarm clock, and that they let him bear the consequences if he chose to oversleep. I assured them that it wouldn't take more than one or two late mornings before he altered his behavior.

The next class meeting Rick and Ellen gave us an update on the morning routine. "Rick and Tommy had picked out an alarm clock with a snooze alarm on it," Ellen reported. "Tommy tried it out the first morning and ended up oversleeping, and consequently was late for school. When he started to complain, I reminded him that I knew he would be more successful tomorrow, but that it was up to him to get himself ready in time. The next day he got out of bed with the first alarm and came down to breakfast in a cheerful mood. I couldn't believe it! He actually seemed to feel good about taking charge of himself." It was beginning to dawn on Tommy that the choice to get up on time did not belong to his parents. This realization is tremendously empowering for a child.

THE GOOD OLD DAYS AND THE BAD OLD DAYS

Parenting in the nineties is challenging, to say the least. The social and scientific progress of the last century has brought us a whole new set of opportunities, and with them, a whole set of problems. In most respects the world is a much better place than it was fifty or a hundred years ago. We live longer. Our health is better. Our children have more freedom than at any other time in history. Because of the social movements of the sixties and the seventies, they are growing up with the belief that "kids are people, too," and deserve to be treated with respect and equality.

THE NEED TO BE NEEDED

The notion that childhood is a time for unencumbered play and learning is a comparatively new idea. It was only two or three generations ago that each child's contribution to the household was essential to the survival of the family as a whole. Splitting firewood, milking the cow, plowing the field, looking after the younger children, were all requirements of daily life. If a child forgot to milk the cow, not only wouldn't there be any milk for breakfast, but the cow's milk might also dry up.

There were real consequences for irresponsible behavior that taught, in no uncertain terms, the importance of cooperation and responsibility.

As we have reaped the benefits of technology, it has become harder for us to find chores for our kids that seem to contribute in a meaningful way.

The truth is, there are no immediately dire consequences if your daughter doesn't take out the garbage. You know it, and she knows it, too. Consequently too often you do the chore yourself—or you let the housekeeper do it, if that's what your lifestyle allows—because somehow that seems easier than going through the trouble of delegating to an untrained or unwilling child. However, although the consequences of not having our children make regular meaningful contributions to our family may not always be immediately apparent, *there are consequences.*

THE CRIPPLING EFFECTS OF THE "I" WORD

Helen and Alex had been divorced for eight years. They have two sons, Hal, ten, and Doug, thirteen. Both of their sons were bright, but were doing poorly in school. Hal had also been sent to the principal's office several times for talking back to his teacher. Neither of the boys was turning in his homework, and their parents were concerned. So the school recommended that they see me for counseling.

After an initial meeting with each parent I met Hal and Doug. I already knew that the boys spent one night a week and every other weekend with their father. I asked them what their visits were like. "When we go to Dad's house, we can do whatever we want," Doug volunteered. "He's a real soft touch!" "Yeah," Hal chimed in. "He lets us go to the video arcade and play games as long as we want to. Or he takes us to the toy store and he buys us new Nintendo cartridges. We get whatever we want."

When I asked them what went on at home, they said, "Our

mom is a lot meaner. She's always nagging us like she's mad all the time."

After several meetings with the boys I got together with Helen and Alex again and asked them what responsibilities their sons have in each household.

"They really don't have to do much at my house," Alex confessed. "We have a housekeeper and she takes care of pretty much everything." Helen's situation sounded different at first glance: "Well, the boys have to do their homework and a few chores, plus getting themselves ready for school." "And they do all that?" I queried. "Uh, well, not exactly," she admitted sheepishly. "When I ask Hal or Doug to help out they get very nasty and refuse. And so a lot of the time I just let it go. They also come into my room every night and bug me to help them with their homework. I always say no at first, then give in and end up spending half the evening on it." I jokingly asked her how she felt about repeating the fourth and seventh grades. "You know, it's true! I'm tired of doing their work for them! But I don't know how to get them to do it themselves."

Both Alex and Helen were indulging their sons to the hilt, although their individual reasons and styles were different. Alex felt guilty because he saw the kids less than Helen, so he tried to make up for it by saying yes to their every whim. Helen saw the need for responsibility but didn't want to seem like the ogre parent, so she tried to set boundaries but ended up caving in—then resenting it, which the kids felt.

With some coaching, both parents started setting limits on the boys' behavior. They established house rules, consequences, and responsibilities that applied uniformly in both households. Helen had a family meeting with her sons and discussed the new setup: Bedtime for Doug would be ten o'clock on school nights and eleven on weekends, and for Hal, nine o'clock on school nights and ten on the weekends. Homework was to be done before they could go out to play. "I will only help you with your homework when I know that you have made an effort to answer the questions on your own," she said firmly. "And I want to know about it ahead of time. Otherwise, you're on your own. You will each be asked to set and clear the table every other night. From now on, if you are asked to do something and you refuse or I have to ask you more than twice, there will be a consequence such as no TV for the day, no Nintendo, or having to stay in after school."

Her sons were shocked and furious. "You can't do that!" Doug wailed "Why do we have so many rules?" Helen stood firm. "I'm tired of you not doing what is expected of you, and I am concerned about how you will learn about taking responsibility if I don't start teaching you."

Helen reported several occasions when her sons tested her on the limits. She was driving them to soccer practice, and Doug was whining and fighting with Hal in the backseat. "I want you to stop yelling," she said quietly. "It's hard for me to concentrate on driving with all this racket going on." Both Hal and Doug ignored her. So, without another word, Helen pulled the car over to the side of the road and refused to drive any further until the boys followed her request. Within minutes they stopped the noise, and Helen got back on the road. It only took a few incidents like this one for her kids to realize that she meant business.

Alex had a similar talk with the boys, and at first they were shocked when they spent the weekend at his house and he adamantly refused to take them to the video arcade. But once they realized that no amount of begging and pleading was going to change Alex's mind, they gave up and began to cooperate with the new limits. Within a few months the boys had settled down. Things at school had improved, and both parents were feeling better about the situation.

Affluence is not inherently bad. But it means that we have to work a lot harder to find ways for our children to see the connection between hard work and privileges.

Without self-discipline kids grow up expecting instant gratification. We all know adults who are bright and talented but who never can seem to make that intelligence or talent really work for them because they simply don't know how to successfully cope with the frustration, discomfort, and hard work involved in successfully accomplishing their goals.

One way to start to shift the responsibility back to your children is to allow them to live with the consequences of their decisions. For example, Jamie has signed up for a class in woodworking, and his instructor has given him a list of required materials. He shows his mother, Olga, the list, and she offers to take him to buy the supplies. He refuses, saying, "I don't want to go today, maybe tomorrow." When tomorrow comes, rather than reminding him, Olga allows Jamie to assume the responsibility for making sure he is prepared for class. As difficult as it may be, she bites her tongue and doesn't point out that his class is tomorrow afternoon and he still hasn't gotten his things together.

The following day Jamie leaves for school completely oblivious that he is unprepared, but comes home from school dejected because he wasn't able to participate in the class project. By allowing Jamie to learn this lesson, Olga insures that he will remember to plan better in the future.

Our love for our kids is best demonstrated through our continual encouragement of their growing independence. This process starts at birth and continues throughout childhood. Our kids need the courage to develop their capabilities and self-confidence. We can support them in developing and maintaining this courage.

MOTHERING VS. SMOTHERING

There is a large amount of self-sacrifice inherent in the process of raising children. But when we continually are doing things for our children, we need to consider whether we're doing it for them or whether we just need to feel needed. When we provide services for our kids that aren't really necessary, we may be attempting to give meaning to our own lives through our children.

Let me give you an example from my own life: My daughter, Ama, receives a clothing allowance every six months. This allowance is sufficient for her to buy the basic necessities for school. We were out one Saturday, and she wanted an especially pretty flowered vest that she saw. She came running over to me. "Mom, look how pretty this is. Can I get it?" I asked, "How much money do you have left in your clothing allowance?" She thought for a moment and replied, "Not enough to buy this." My immediate impulse was to say, "Okay, it really is pretty, I'll get it for you." I wanted her to love me and to view me as a generous mom. And there is a certain satisfaction that comes with being the benevolent dispenser of goodies. But knowing my weakness in this area, I restrained myself. And then, before I could give her an answer, she piped up with her own suggestion: "How about if we each pay half, would you be willing to do that?" That seemed like a good compromise. We made a deal about how she would repay me for her half of the vest. We worked out an hourly wage for the time she would spend helping out in the office, doing mailings and sending out tapes. In this way I was able to help her get what she wanted, but she also had an active role in providing it for herself.

THE HELICOPTER PARENT

Have you ever found yourself hovering around your kids, waiting to go into action on a search-and-rescue mission? I call this the "helicopter parent syndrome." You step in and rescue your three-year-old when she pulls on a red plaid skirt with a turquoise striped top. You jump up to settle an argument between your six-year-old and his friend over a toy. You try to save your teenager from making her girlfriend angry instead of allowing her to figure things out for herself. In a lot of cases this hovering is not about love as much as it is about your own worry as to how your children's actions, appearance, and behavior will reflect on *you*.

Take Adam's mom, Denise: Adam, thirteen, had grown up with a mother who was overly responsible, a dyed-in-the-wool helicopter parent. Denise was a delightful woman, but she had quit her job when Adam was born and was looking to her role as a mother for all of her sense of self-worth and self-esteem. Finally, at my suggestion, she had recently taken a part-time job. She was at work when Adam called her on the phone, frantic. "Mom, Mrs. Williams is outside waiting to take me to baseball practice, and I can't find my glove! Do you know where it is?" Denise started to jump into her search-and-rescue mode: "Have you looked in your brother's room? Did you look in the family room? How about in the backyard?" Suddenly, in the midst of all this rescuing, a light bulb went off in her head. She realized in a flash that all this "help" was not so much for Adam as it was because she didn't want Mrs. Williams to think badly of her son (or of *her*, worse yet!). And all at once Denise saw how ridiculous this was. So she took a breath then said calmly, "Adam, it's your mitt. You're responsible for keeping track of it. I hope you can find it." And she hung up the phone.

A rule of thumb is: Don't do for your kids what they can do for themselves. We need to learn to do the opposite of the old adage "Don't just stand there, do something." We need to "don't do anything, just stand there," and patiently allow our kids to develop their "struggle muscle."

Kids who haven't had the occasion to *practice* making choices in the safety of their family will be thrown completely for a loop when they enter the adult world. I am not suggesting that you abandon your children and allow them to make *all* of the decisions in their lives. They need your guidance. The trick is to guide with a light—rather than a heavy—hand.

The time Ama called me from school in a panic is a perfect example. One of her teachers had offered a job baby-sitting her three-year-old daughter three days a week. "Mom, what should I do?" she whispered frantically into the phone. "I don't know what to say. I'd like to earn the extra money and to help her out, but it would mean I wouldn't have much time to hang out with my friends." Obviously she wanted my help, but I decided that rather than give her my opinion, I would help her sort out her own dilemma. So I threw the question back to her: "What do *you* want to do?" I asked. "Well," she said, "I could really use the extra money and I'd like to help Ms. Petrick out, but it would mean that I'd have less time to spend with my friends and for my homework." I then asked her, "What's more important to you right now?" She thought for a minute. "I guess I really don't want to do it," she replied finally.

It would have been so easy for me to have jumped in and told Ama what to do. But she wouldn't have had the experience of weighing out the pros and cons of the situation and evaluating what was best for her. In this case I guided Ama through the decision-making process. However, that was a year ago, and now, when similar situations arise, she is usually able to go through the process on her own.

DEVELOPING CAPABLE KIDS

Children are born motivated to learn, grow, and contribute. Their natural tendency is to want to feel like a significant member of their family. By our own responses to those budding tendencies, we will either encourage or discourage their feelings of capability.

Jonathon, two, wants to help his mother set the dinner table. His mother says to him, "You're too little to help, you'll break the plates." Rather than redirecting his desire to help by suggesting that he put on the silverware or the napkins, instead she inadvertently ends up bruising her child's sense of confidence in his growing ability.

Three-year-old Audrey was constantly bugging her mother, Irene, to let her help with the daily chores around her house. "I want to do it, Mommy," she would say. "Let me help." But her mother would continually reply, "You're too little to help. Go and play now, or go and watch your video." Unintentionally Audrey's mother started to undermine her sense of capability. If our kids get the continual message "You're too little; it's too hard for you; wait until you get older," they begin to lose their motivation to participate in family activities.

When I met Audrey, she was a teenager. Her mother had come to me in frustration because Audrey was so uncooperative when it came to chores. Her routine response when asked to help would be, "No, Mom, I'm busy watching my show!" or "Not right now, Mom, I'm playing with my friends." At times she would even ignore her mother completely. It was only after I had talked with both mother and daughter at length that it came to light how many times Irene had discouraged Audrey from helping as a young child. It took far more time and effort to undo this negative training than it would have to encourage Audrey in those early years.

Suppose your five-year-old grabs the egg carton to help you unload the groceries and you grab it from her yelling, "Don't do that! Eggs break easily. You better wait until you get bigger to help." What impact do you think this kind of message will have? The fact is, young children are capable of handling eggs carefully and putting them away if they are just given a little help and instruction. The worst thing that could happen is that you'd have a few broken eggs!

When our children receive too large a dose of discouragement, they lose their motivation to try. They begin developing an I-can't-do-it-so-why-try attitude, and lack the faith in their ability to contribute. When they are allowed to help with everyday chores, they glow with pride for having done a job well and seeing how pleased you are with their accomplishments.

TAKE TIME FOR TEACHING

It's true that our children can't do things as well as we can initially. Jay, eleven, decided he would cook dinner for his family on Mother's Day. Dinnertime rolled around, and his mother, Lila, asked, "What have you planned for dinner?" He said, "I don't know yet." At that moment it would have been so tempting for Lila to have taken over, but her goal was to support Jay in accomplishing what he set out to do. She made a few suggestions, and then left him in the kitchen. Two hours later the kitchen looked as if a hurricane had hit it, but Jay had made spaghetti and a salad. As he brought the food to the table, he was nearly floating with pride for having done something for his family and having mastered a new skill. We have to be willing to overlook the outcome of some jobs in order for our kids to develop their capability.

The only way our kids can become contributing family members is if we teach them how to make their beds, do the laundry, operate the vacuum cleaner, load the dishwasher, and put away the groceries. Once we have instructed them in the various chores, they can participate in meaningful ways. And it will lighten your load as well.

For years Carla thought it was her job to do the grocery shopping, haul the countless bags into the house, and then carefully put all the food away in its appointed places. After having done this for what seemed like an eternity, she resented the fact that no one offered to help her. Then one day it dawned on her that she had been unwilling to give up the control of how the food was put away. As a result she continued to do it *all* herself. With the coaching of other parents in my class, she decided that rather than go on feeling angry and resentful, she would enlist the support of her children.

Carla discussed the problem with her family one night over dinner, and asked her two children Roger, seven, and Jordan, nine, to come out and help carry in the groceries next time she made a run to the market. She said that she would show them how to unload the food. It took a few trips to the store before Carla felt comfortable letting her kids put the groceries away on their own. But when she took time to guide them, she found they were quite willing to cooperate. "I can't believe I waited so long to do this," she laughed when she reported her success to the class. "I feel so relieved having my kids pitch in.

And what's even more amazing is that they seem delighted with how well they can do the job."

When we appreciate our kids' efforts, no matter how small, at contributing to our family, we are supporting them in feeling more competent and capable. As adults, we all want to feel like valuable people who make contributions to our children and to life in general. This is also true of our kids. When we stop long enough to guide and train them in ways they can contribute, we help them add polish and shine to their self-esteem both now and later as they grow.

Teaching Tips

Our children aren't instant learners. They need time and practice to learn new skills.

There are several steps that will make teaching your child a new skill go more smoothly.

1. Make Special Time for Teaching. The morning rush or dinnertime, when you are feeling stressed, aren't good times to begin teaching your kids how to make their beds, get dressed, or peel carrots. The pressure of the moment, added to our sense of impatience, can produce discouragement and rebellion in our kids. We need to set aside a special time specifically for teaching. This should be a time when you are willing to work patiently with your child in learning a new skill.

2. Practice Makes Excellence. Learning a new skill takes time and repeated practice. Don't make critical remarks when your children make a mistake. Let your children practice a new skill while you watch. Offer help if they can't accomplish the job on their own: "You've made a good start making your bed. Can I show you how to straighten out the covers?"

3. An Encouraging Attitude Fosters Learning. An attitude of patience and confidence in our children's growing ability to learn supports the learning process. "I can see how hard you're working," or "Try again, you almost have it," or "I bet you feel good about learning to tie your shoes" can make the learning process enjoyable, and one in which our kids feel supported and appreciated for their efforts.

3. Make It Fun. You can teach your child table manners by having an afternoon tea party. Learning to tie shoes or getting dressed can be done with dolls or by making a button board (taking an old blouse with large buttonholes and tacking it onto a piece of cardboard). The point is to enjoy the learning process and your time together.

4. Encourage Togetherness. Young children are more motivated to do things for themselves if we are in the same room with them. We can be nearby and doing separate things. At times it is more effective to make a joint project out of folding the laundry or cleaning up the playroom. Young children may need you to get them started and to check back with them periodically as they learn a new skill.

5. Provide Opportunities for Learning. Sometimes it takes a bit of creative thinking to find good opportunities for our kids to learn. It really requires changing our habits from doing something completely ourselves to taking the time to notice which tasks we can begin to turn over to our children.

6. Express Appreciation. Let your kids know that you recognize and appreciate their efforts and newly acquired skills: "Thanks for folding the laundry"; "I can see you worked really hard at setting the table, thanks"; or, "I felt really good when I walked into the kitchen this morning and you had wiped off the counters."

Our children deserve a training period that leads to a sense of capability and personal mastery.

Exercise: Learning Something New. I have done this exercise numerous times with parents in my classes, and they invariably return with helpful insights that they can apply in teaching their kids new skills. One mother realized that when she was a little girl her mother seldom allowed her to do anything on her own. She recalled being asked to set the table and having her mother stand over her, shouting commands about where everything needed to be put.

By remembering this and other experiences, she understood why she had so little self-confidence and had difficulty letting her son try things by himself.

Use this exercise as a tool to discover what you experienced as a child and how you can learn both from the mistakes that were made as well as what encouraged and motivated you.

Recall a time when one of your parents taught you a new skill. Take a moment and remember the situation in as much detail as possible, using this list as an example.[1]

Whom were you with?_____

What were they teaching you?_____

_____

How did you feel about your parent then?_____

_____

How did you feel about yourself?_____

_____

What did they do that was supportive and encouraging of your efforts?_____

_____

What did they do that discouraged you or inhibited your efforts?

_____

What can you learn from this experience that you can now apply to teaching your own children?_____

_____

Make a list of everything you are currently doing for your children. Then go down the list and check off those things that they can do for themselves. Examples: dressing them, making their beds, tying their shoes, picking up their toys, etc. This week choose *one* thing from your list that you are going to let your child do for herself. If it is a new skill, follow the guidelines outlined in the earlier section "Take Time for Teaching."

THE LANGUAGE OF RESPONSIBILITY

"You knew you were supposed to come home right after school, and you're an hour late. You're grounded for the rest of the week." "I told you not to leave your bike on the front lawn. No wonder it got stolen. That was really using your smarts!" "You knew what would happen if you didn't turn in your English homework!" We've seen that encouraging responsibility in our kids is an essential part of parenting. Moreover, we encourage responsibility not only through our actions and the things we say, but also through the way we say what we say. All of the above statements are phrased in such a manner that they encourage blame, not self-discipline. However, by training ourselves to use what I call "the language of responsibility," we can encourage our kids to assume more rather than less responsibility for themselves and their actions.

For example, we foster responsibility in our kids when we ask clear questions, make direct requests, and ask questions that require them to stop and think about their behavior and its consequences. Through using the language of responsibility we give our kids the essential message "You choose; you decide; it's up to you."

Guidelines for Using the Language of Responsibility
1. Put the responsibility for decision-making or problem-solving back on your child. Ask, "How are you going to handle this situation?" Inquire how he feels about his grades before offering your opinion. Let's say your child walks in the door and hands you his report card. He got three

"A"s, two "C"s, and a "D" in math. Rather than jumping on his case, ask him, "How do you feel about your grades?" Child: "Not too great. I worked very hard in most of my subjects, but I really slacked off in math. I want to bring up my grade before the next semester." Kids who are given the chance to form their own opinions about their actions learn to make decisions effectively and are better problem-solvers.

2. *Help your child to realize her choices and the resulting consequences.* Child: "I can't go to baseball practice today. I'm too tired." Parent: "What do you think will happen if you don't go?" Child: "I might get kicked off the team." Parent: "Well, how will you feel if that happens?"

3. *Remove self-imposed limits.* Many times our kids act as though there is a force beyond their control that prevents them from doing certain things, when in reality it is their own decisions. Child: "It's impossible for me to finish this homework." Parent: "What's stopping you?" Or, "Is it really impossible, or just difficult?" Child: "I can't pick up all these toys." Parent: "Is it that you can't, or that you don't want to?"

4. *Encourage reality-based thinking.* Sometimes our children make global generalizations that exaggerate the situation: "You always," "You never." We can help our kids by bringing in a less desperate, more realistic tone. If we challenge them to think about the present reality and not their imagined fantasy, this teaches them how to better respond to the actual situation at hand rather than merely their emotions about the situation. Child: "I always have to set the table! You never make Sid help!" Parent: "Who set the table last night?" Child: "You're mean. You never let me stay up late." Parent: "It seems like it was only last week that you stayed up past your bedtime to watch that PBS special."

5. *Use cause-and-effect language.* We can help our children take responsibility for their feelings and actions by

identifying their reaction to another person's behavior. Child: "Gilda really makes me mad." Parent: "What is it that she does that upsets you?" Child: "Gilda made me laugh during PE and got me benched." Parent: "How is Gilda's behavior related to your getting benched?" This approach forces our kids to look at their own contribution to the experience. The event may be caused by another person, but the child needs to know that his response is his own choice.

6. *When in doubt, have them check it out.* Children often pretend to know what other people are thinking, what their intentions are, or what the motivation is behind another person's actions. For example, your child may say, "Drew hates me." Suppose you respond with something like, "What has he done that makes you think he doesn't like you?" Then you teach him to be actively involved in clarifying the situation for himself. If your daughter says, "My teacher thinks I'm stupid" and you try and convince her otherwise, you don't help her to check out her perceptions and discover the truth. If instead you say, "What does she do that causes you to believe that?" you encourage her to look further and thus perhaps arrive at a different conclusion. By asking, you cause her to think. Child: "Well, she never calls on me in class." Parent: "Is it possible that she may have overlooked you? Why don't you talk with her?" This kind of interaction supports children in considering another possibility and trains them to check things out.

7. *Ask kids "What" questions rather than "Why" questions.* "What" questions cause them to stop, identify, and evaluate their behavior. "What are you doing?" or "What are you supposed to be doing?" rather than "Why haven't you picked up your toys?" will force the child to stop what she is doing and start to think about what she is supposed to do. Parent: "What are you doing?" Child: "Watching TV." Parent: "What are you supposed to be doing?" Child:

"Getting ready for bed." Parent: "What happens when you don't put your toys away when you finish playing with them?" Child: "They get taken away for two days."

8. *Help kids remember the rules themselves.* Instead of telling your child the rule, you can ask him a question that supports him in taking responsibility for knowing the rule himself. Parent: "What's the rule about coming home after school?" Child: "I'm supposed to come straight home, and if you're not here, I'm supposed to leave you a note." Parent: "What's the rule about eating just before dinner?" Child: "No snacks right before dinner." Parent: "When can you have snacks?" Child: "When I get home from school and after dinner." When you want to clarify rules, do it in three steps: 1) Clearly state the rule; 2) Ask your child to restate the rule; and 3) Ask your child to apply the rule.

9. *Ask questions that are open-ended rather than closed.* For example: "Are you having a good time?," "Did you have a good day?," or "Did you like the movie?" are closed questions. They only require a yes or no answer. "What things did you enjoy doing?" is open-ended, as is, "What was good about your day?" or "Tell me about your favorite part of the movie."

Open-ended questions invite your children to engage in a dialogue with you. They allow your kids to give more thoughtful responses.

The more we can allow our children to do things for themselves, the more strongly we communicate the message, "I believe in your ability and growing skills." As you get in the habit of using the language of responsibility, you'll be able to see tangible evidence of your children's growing sense of independence. When we ask our children for their ideas and suggestions, we are often surprised by the creative practical solutions they present. Our kids are more likely to follow through with the solutions when they have helped create them.

INNER DIRECTION IS THE MAGIC WORD

"Inner direction" is another way of saying self-motivated, self-guided. Internally directed people believe that there is a direct correlation between what I do and what happens to me. They realize that improving their life is largely due to the decisions they make and the amount of effort they invest in any given situation. Internally motivated people enjoy other people's approval, but don't rely on it for their own happiness. When they are successful, they take credit for their accomplishments, knowing that their decisions and effort contributed to their achievement.

The following is a wonderful story that I've always felt perfectly sums up the issue of inner direction:

There once was an energetic young monkey who lived in the same jungle as an aging male monkey. The old one was a veteran of so many battles that he lacked all but two toes on his left foot and thus was known to the other members of the monkey colony as "Two Toes." One sunny day as the monkeys gathered at the clearing near the river, Two Toes stood and watched as the young monkey ran in circles chasing his tail. At first Two Toes made no comment. But as the afternoon waned and the young monkey persisted with this odd tail-chasing behavior, the older monkey's curiosity was piqued. He strolled over for a closer look. "What on earth are you doing, child?" he chattered in monkey dialect. The young monkey stopped in surprise. "I've just returned from the Monkey Philosophic Academy," he answered confidently, "and I learned two wonderful things there. One, that the most important thing in the world for a monkey is happiness, and two, that happiness is always in one's tail. So," concluded the young monkey with a self-important twitch of the tail in question, "obviously I'm going to keep chasing my tail, because as soon as I catch it, I'm going to get a taste of true happiness."

Two Toes thought this over for a moment before he finally responded. "Well, I didn't have the same benefits that you did of going to the Monkey Philosophic Academy," he said in the slow way he always spoke, "but I've been out and around in this jungle for quite a few years, and I do believe you're right that true happiness is in our tails. However, the main difference between you and me is that I found that if I go about my business and enjoy my life, my tail always manages to follow after me wherever I go."[2]

The message in this story is simple, but, I believe, absolutely crucial for us to pass on to our children: Happiness cannot be pursued directly. However, if one is truly able to go about one's business in a responsible and inner-directed fashion, happiness will follow.

Chapter 8
FACING THE *D*-WORD

"Virtue isn't hereditary, it has to be taught."
—Thomas Jefferson

Have you ever felt as though your children were out to get you? As if their goal in life were to make you miserable? It's helpful to recognize that there is a difference between your children's agenda and your own. They really don't misbehave just to torture you. A certain amount of conflict between you and your children is normal and necessary. This is due to their job description: to explore this strange new world, and to seek out ways of making life interesting.

Let's say you are standing in line for the movies and your five-year-old daughter is having a great time running up and down the line, weaving in and out of people's legs and shrieking with enjoyment. What you want is for your daughter to stand quietly with you and behave herself; and what she wants to do is to make this boring situation entertaining. The discrepancy in job descriptions naturally leads to conflict. The way you deal with these conflicts. determines whether the discipline is effective or harmful.

FACING THE *D*-WORD

I was walking around a lake the other day and stopped to watch a turtle and her baby basking in the sun. As I looked around the lake, I noticed that all of the newly planted trees had two stakes driven into the ground next to them. These stakes were to protect the young saplings from the wind as they were developing. The young trees also had rubber hoops surrounding them that were attached to the stakes. These hoops were loose enough to allow the trees to move within limits, yet firm enough to protect them as they developed. This is how discipline works.

When a tree matures, its root system deepens and its trunk becomes stronger, and we can remove the stakes—but not until that time. Without the protection of the stakes the young trees could grow crooked or bent, or even break altogether when a storm comes.

Our children are much like these young trees. One of our functions as parents is to provide firm yet gentle guidelines for them as they grow. As they develop and mature, we can remove the stakes to allow them to experience themselves as independent, responsible, self-disciplined adults. When we raise our children with firm, clear guidelines, we are teaching them how to function within a democratic society in which freedom has limitations. As we set and maintain limits for our children, we are teaching them how to be successful and productive adults.

To most of us, the *D*-word means being spanked, yelled at, or banished to our room. The very word causes many us to cringe, remembering our own childhoods, when our parents would threaten us with, "I'll wash your mouth out with soap young lady," or "You just wait until your father gets home, then you'll really be sorry!" We confuse discipline with punishment, but the words have very different meanings. Punishment can damage a child's spirit, whereas discipline comes from the Greek word *disciplina,* which means "to teach" or "to lead." In the truest sense of the word we are teaching our children how to lead themselves, in other words to be self-disciplined.

We aren't always going to be with our kids, so we want them to have a strong, responsible inner voice that will lead them to make choices in their own best interest. In order for this internal structure to evolve, we have to discipline our children in a way that respects their individuality and humanity.

Yet when we set firm boundaries, we provide them with a sense of safety and security. When we discipline our children with love, the messages we give are, "I care too much about you to let you act inappropriately" and "I care enough about you to take the time and effort to teach you how to behave."

WHY DO CHILDREN MISBEHAVE?

One of the main reasons children misbehave is to get their parents' attention. The kind of attention they usually get is negative attention, in the form of anger and disapproval. But to a child this is better than no attention at all. This is why I'll remind you over and over to comment on the things your children do well, or the behaviors you want to see, and to spend time hanging out with your kids. This way they are less likely to feel they have to act out to get noticed. Keep in mind as you discipline your children that a second reason they misbehave is that your kids do not have as developed a conscience as you do. It is your job to guide them until they develop one of their own.

THE POWER OF PARENTHOOD

In the old days the models for conflict resolution were based on submission and inequality. Mom obeyed Dad (or looked as if she did), and the children obeyed them both. The underlying philosophy was, "It's my way or the highway." The father was the commander in chief, and everyone was afraid to challenge his authority. Authoritarian parenting was based on threats, power, and control. It worked, but at a very high price. More recently we have discovered that cooperation works much better than control, because, among other reasons, when you control your children's behavior with power and authority, the behavior usually lasts about as long as the authority figure is present.

Remember when you were in school and you had a teacher whom you fondly called the "drill sergeant"? You know the kind; when he walked into the room, everyone became silent and held their breath. In seventh grade I had a science teacher named Mr. Parasugo. He dressed and acted like a sergeant in the Marine Corps. When he came into the classroom, everyone became silent and sat up straight in our desks. No one dared make a peep while he was in our presence. However, the moment Mr. Parasugo walked out of the classroom—say, if he was called to the office—kids started screaming, throwing spitballs and paper airplanes, and climbing over chairs. Chaos reigned during the entire time Mr. Parasugo was away.

The authoritarian method has been part of our heritage for so long that many people still consider it to be the only bona fide form of discipline. Some of us, although we don't think of ourselves as authoritarian, may use more subtle forms of authoritarianism than we would care to admit. However, using the authoritarian approach—whether overt or covert—can have negative consequences. When children grow up with excessive strictness, they feel powerless. These kids often seek to take back power through self-destructive rebellion against their parents' iron-fisted rule.

My nineteen-year-old client Janet is a perfect example. She had got into the habit of lying to her parents. "We've been lied to so many times," they finally confessed to me in exasperation, "that we don't believe *anything* Janet tells us now."

In the course of one of our conversations Janet told me about the first time she remembered lying to her father. "My dad was bugged that I left my clothes on the floor," she explained. "He asked me to clean up my room, and I was in a hurry. My best friend, Mindy, was over, and we were on our way out to a party, so I shoved everything under my bed. After I left, he came into my room and found my clothes shoved under my bed. That night when I got home from the party, he asked me to come into my room. He had dragged everything out from under my bed, and he asked me to pick out one outfit. Then he gathered up the rest of my clothes, stuffed them into a big black plastic garbage bag, and put them out in the garage. He said that the outfit I had chosen was the only thing I could wear for the rest of the week. I begged, cried, and pleaded with him, but he wouldn't change his mind. At first I couldn't believe it. I wore the outfit the next day, but I felt so self-conscious about what the kids were going to say if I showed up day after day wearing the same thing that I snuck some clothes out of the house in my backpack and changed before I got to school. I kept sneaking clothes every day that week and lying to my dad when he asked me about it. It was the only way I could keep from being teased."

This was just the beginning of Janet's career of stealing, lying, cutting classes, and drinking with her friends, all actions that damaged her self-esteem. And yet, ironically, those first lies were an attempt to *preserve* her self-esteem in the face of her father's power play.

When parents use authoritarian methods, they assume total responsibility for their children's behavior. There is very little room for children to question, think for themselves, to disagree, or to challenge. The worst aspect of this approach is that it damages your children's sense of self-worth. It is a daily reminder that we don't trust our children's ability to use good judgment or to act cooperatively. The underlying feeling they are left with is, "My ideas must not be very good. I guess I can't trust myself. I need someone older and wiser to make my decisions for me." Many parents refuse to give up the "Do it my way or else" position (which often includes spanking), thinking mistakenly that permissiveness is the only alternative.

ALL SHE NEEDS IS A GOOD SPANKING!

Most of us know intuitively that spanking isn't a humane tool for disciplining our children, but when we get frustrated and can't get our children to change, we use it as a last resort.

And Our Sensitive Parent of the Year Award Goes To . . .

In his monthly newsletter entitled *Focus on the Family*, Dr. James Dobson gives the following advice to a woman who asked what she can do when her three-year-old son refuses to stay in bed at night. He replied, "I would suggest that the youngster be placed in bed and given a little speech, such as, 'Johnny, this time Mommie means business. Are you listening to me? Do not get out of bed.' Then when Johnny's feet touch the floor, give him a swat on the legs with a small switch. Put the switch on his dresser where he can see it, and promise him one more stroke if he gets up again."

According to a Harris Poll released in the summer of 1989, today, 86 percent of Americans still spank their children, and 60 percent of those parents spank their children every week. These parents, when questioned, say that they don't want to, but do so because they feel that they have no other choice.[1]

Parents resort to spanking because it works in the short run. It makes an indelible impact. But in the long term it has severe consequences. Because we generally spank both to change our child's behavior *and* to get out our own frustration, this combination of power and anger doesn't make children want to improve. It only creates resentment and a desire for revenge.

Think about it. How would you feel if someone hit you?

You would want to hit back, right? You'd want to retaliate for the hurt and humiliation. Parents who hit their children teach them that the way to get their needs met is to use physical force over someone weaker than they. Children who are hit will hit other children. They have no way to differentiate that it's okay for Mom or Dad to hit me, but it's not okay for me to hit other kids. Furthermore, all the studies have conclusively demonstrated that children who are hit frequently and abusively almost always are abusive parents. We live in a culture where all too often the use of power and violence is employed as a way to solve problems. This is not a way of living that any of us want to perpetuate with our children. Maybe it will take several generations of people who refuse to spank or hit their children to break the cycle. Then perhaps our grandchildren can grow up in a sane world.

I know that a lot of you feel that spanking is a necessity. Unfortunately spanking is habit-forming; once you start, it's hard to stop. Plus, each time you use it, it's less and less effective, so over a period of time, you're likely to find yourself spanking more frequently. Why start in the first place? What I'd like to suggest is that although spanking works in the short run, there are far better long-range methods that won't generate fear and resentment in your kids and leave you feeling like a storm trooper.

OLD FAVORITES

Throughout time we have stumbled upon many ineffective ways of disciplining our children. Here are four of my perennial favorites: Screaming at the top of your lungs, threatening your children, name-calling, and the Darth Vader approach.

Screaming at the top of your lungs is an old standard. Your lungs get a workout, while your blood pressure goes through the roof. Once your throat feels sore from yelling and you realize that yelling hasn't worked, you usually move into *threat-*

ening your children: "If you don't stop that right now, you'll really be sorry!" This generally doesn't work, either, so you may resort to *name-calling*: "You're a spoiled brat!"

Then there's the ultimate in authoritarian parenting: *The Darth Vader approach*. This goes in steps. First, you make the assumption that good parents never get angry. Second, you ask your kid at least ten times to do something while holding in your anger.

I would personally do this until I finally exploded and went berserk. I'd jump up from my chair, red in the face, with my eyes bulging out of my head and race over to Ama at top speed with my arms extended as if I were going to strangle her. This did produce results. It always got her to move, and she did take me more seriously. But there is a danger that goes along with this method. If your friends catch you doing this, they'll probably think you're crazy; and your children will become absolutely terrified of you.

PERMISSIVE PARENTING: THE OTHER EXTREME

Just as it is with authoritarian parenting, even if you don't consider yourself a permissive parent, you may under stress use permissive methods. Take for example the *wishy-washy approach*. I became so expert at this one that it took several years to break myself of the habit. This is when you say no, but you don't really mean it. You say it more like a question than a statement: "No, okay?"

My daughter could always smell my guilt and indecisiveness a mile away. She would push me and push me, knowing that if she pushed long and hard enough, I would eventually give in and say, "Okay, okay, go ahead, but just this one time, now leave me alone!" This approach accomplishes several things: Your child learns that if she bugs you long enough, you'll give in; and you end up with a case of terminal frustration and

THE MAGIC OF ENCOURAGEMENT

feelings of inadequacy for having given in and let a mere child push you around. What I'd then do was to go yell at my husband while this little tyrant ran our household.

Children are very pragmatic: They only do what works. Let's say you take your son to the grocery store and he throws a temper tantrum in the checkout line, screaming, "Mommy, I want a candy bar." You finally give in to his demands to get him to shut up. In doing so, you are teaching him that if he yells long enough and loud enough, you will give in. Many parents feel intimidated by their misbehaving children, especially in public, and we end up "pretzeling" ourselves to get our kids to behave. We need to separate our sense of self-worth from what other people may think of us. Remember, these people are strangers, and you may never see them again. Besides it's your son, not you, who is causing the commotion. One father reported to me that when his daughter threw a fit in the market, he very matter-of-factly called people over to watch her. She was so shocked that she stopped and never did it again. She learned that that behavior was not going to get her what she wanted, and she would have to find another way of behaving with her father.

Parents who are habitually permissive are often reacting against overly strict or controlling methods used by their own parents. They are terrified of setting firm limits for fear that they will harm their children's psychological development. And usually underlying this is the fear that their children won't love them anymore. Well, let's set the record straight once and for all: Kids continue to love you even when you set firm limits. They may not like what you say to them all the time, but they feel safe and secure knowing what the rules are and what you expect of them. When children are allowed to misbehave, they feel uncomfortable inside. It not only makes them feel insecure, it also teaches kids to get their needs met through manipulating others. Long-term studies have demonstrated that a permissive method of discipline, by which parents accept inappropriate behavior from their kids, results in children who lack a sense of responsibility and capability, and who become overly dependent on adults. They are poor achievers and problem-solvers. As they get older, they are likely to become users and manipulators, because parents have bailed them out from experiencing any negative consequences from their behavior. Interestingly several studies show that children who grow up with parents who do not set and firmly maintain limits and consequences believe that their parents don't really love them.

DEMOCRATIC PARENTING

The democratic approach is somewhere between the authoritarian and the permissive methods. The parents who use this method are leaders who encourage cooperation and learning. The rights and needs of others are respected, and each family member is an equal who is just as valuable and as important as everyone else. The focus in a democratic family is on balancing the rights and responsibilities of each person. The democratic method is based on freedom within limits, and teaches children how to function within a democratic society. The hallmark of a democratic home is mutual respect and involvement. Parents share power with their kids and work together to establish rules and responsibilities. In these homes parents have high expectations of their children and work at motivating them through using encouragement for their efforts and accomplishments. There is a balance between firmness and kindness. Rules are clearly defined and enforced in an attitude of dignity and mutual respect.

We have seen over the years that children who have high self-esteem come from families who share power and use democratic methods of discipline. These children are more capable of thinking on their own, tend to be more considerate of others, and are more independent than children raised in either permissive or authoritarian homes. Children want and

THE MAGIC OF ENCOURAGEMENT

need to be corrected when they misbehave. If you don't, they feel unloved, insecure, and unworthy. Yet children who are raised in homes in which their opinions are respected have less of a need to rebel against authority when they get older. This is because their self-esteem remains intact.

Our society requires that individuals make choices and decisions and that they be responsible for the consequences of their actions. Our children will be asked to make thousands of decisions in the course of their lives, and will be held accountable for those choices. And we won't be there to help them.

However, if we have allowed them to make choices and to live with the consequences of their choices, they will be prepared to make courageous, life-enhancing decisions for themselves. Isn't that what we want for our children, for them to be able to face life's challenges with courage and clarity? When you discipline your children with respect, kindness, and firmness, they internalize these qualities and are better able to incorporate them into their everyday interactions as they grow.

Exercise: Discipline Inventory. If you can remember how you felt as a child when you were disciplined, you will understand your own kids better. You can benefit not only from the mistakes your parents made, but also from what they did that was effective. Take a few minutes to answer the following questions. This exercise can be done alone or be shared with your partner or a friend. It can stimulate an interesting discussion.

1. How was discipline handled in your family when you were growing up?————————————————————

————————————————————————————

2. Who did most of the disciplining?————————————

————————————————————————————

3. How did you feel when you were disciplined?——————

————————————————————————————

4. How do you feel about disciplining your children?_____

_____

5. What methods are you currently using to discipline your kids?

_____

_____

6. How effective do you feel in disciplining your kids?

_____

_____

7. What improvements would you like to make?_____

_____

By taking the time to recall your own experiences as a child, you can better understand and evaluate your old conditioned responses. Once you do this sorting process, you will be able to make genuine changes and learn new tools to handle discipline more effectively in your own families.

Chapter 9
DISCIPLINE WITH LOVE: A PRACTICAL GUIDE

"Every pearl is the result of an oyster's victory over an irritation."
—Anonymous

Two-year-old Tory says no to almost everything her mother asks her to do. "Time to pick up your toys." "No." "You have to get dressed now." "No." "It's time to go to sleep." "No." "I'm at the end of my rope," says her nice, well-meaning mother. "There are days when I think one of us just has to go."

Matt, five, interrupts all the time. Like the afternoon his mother had a friend over for lunch. "Matt must have interrupted our conversation at least ten times," sighed his mother in exasperation. "He has his own agenda, and he acts as if everything should center on him. It doesn't seem to matter where we are or who's talking, he constantly interrupts. Sometimes I want to scream, 'Shut up and leave me alone!' "

Jessica, ten, won't do her homework. Jason, thirteen, argues every time he's asked to do household chores. Samantha, seventeen, leaves her clothes, books, and all manner of other messes strewn around the house.

Do any of these situations sound familiar? Most of us have

dealt with similar problems at one time or another. No matter what the ages of our children, they each offer different disciplinary challenges. Kids somehow always manage to challenge our efforts at maintaining order, developing responsibility, and building character.

It's not surprising that in every one of my seminars parents inevitably ask, "How can I get my child to go to bed?" "What do I do when my son won't get dressed in the morning?" "What do I do when my kids fight?" "How do I get my kids to listen to me?" Discipline is a mystery to most parents. In absolutely every class I teach, the majority of the parents who attend express how powerless they feel in dealing with their kids' misbehavior.

Discipline is difficult, but it's even more so if it results in negative feelings between you and your children. You don't want to leave them feeling bad about themselves. What you want is to leave them with a clear understanding of what is expected of them. To accomplish this goal, we don't have to humiliate or harm our children's self esteem or bodies. We can guide our kids with love and firmness toward the goal of self-discipline.

We discussed an overview of democratic discipline in the previous chapter. Now, it's time to learn how to implement these ideas.

COMMITMENT AND CARING: THE BOTTOM LINE

There is no magic formula that will answer all of your disciplinary questions. There isn't one perfect way to discipline your kids. Nor is every method going to work with every child or in every situation. But what we *can* do is to commit ourselves to a positive approach to discipline. One that includes respect, clearly defined expectations, limits, reasonable consequences, and earned privileges.

TWELVE STEPS TO EFFECTIVE DISCIPLINE

1. Plan ahead.
2. Ignore what isn't really important to you.
3. Take time to think before acting or reacting.
4. Encourage cooperation.
5. Hold a positive expectation.
6. Communicate clearly and concisely.
7. Give children choices.
8. Speak assertively.
9. Be consistent.
10. Use natural or logical consequences.
11. Discuss the issue calmly.
12. Forgive and forget.

Each of the methods can be used in daily situations with children of all ages.

Step 1: Plan ahead. Here is an example of what can happen when we don't anticipate situations. Four-year-old Julie was on the way to the market with her mother, Megan. Halfway between home and the store Julie started chanting:

"I want a new toy, Mom."

"Not today, Julie. You just got a new toy last week."

"I want a toy."

"Not today."

"I want a toy!"

Julie proceeded to throw a temper tantrum, and refused to go into the store. If Megan had thought through this situation ahead of time, she could have discussed where they were going and what they were going to buy before they left home. In one of my classes we discussed what had gone wrong and how she might prevent future scenes with Julie. The next time she was going to the store, Megan prepared Julie for what they were going to do. "Julie, we're going to go to the market in a little while to buy groceries." When Julie immediately began her litany—"I want candy, Mommy!"—Megan could explain to her daughter what she would and wouldn't do. "I know you like to get a treat when we go shopping, but I'm not buying any candy today. You can get a frozen yogurt on the way home instead." We can defuse potentially frustrating situations for our children by letting them know ahead of time what to expect, and just what we will and will not do.

ONE THING AT A TIME

Angela came into one of my seminars complaining that her daughter Randi had the telephone permanently attached to her head. "She leaves her books and clothes all over the house," sighed Angela. "She doesn't do her chores, her room is a mess, and she leaves her homework until the last minute." I asked Angela what had she tried up to this point. She said she was constantly reminding Randi of all the things she was doing wrong. This is better known as nagging. I asked her how effective this had been. She said, "Randi just tunes me out, and things get worse." Randi had become "parent deaf."

I suggested that Angela choose *one* specific area to work on at a time. Otherwise, it is too overwhelming for both parent and child. What did she want changed, and what should be the consequences if Randi didn't cooperate? For example, if Angela's first priority was to change Randi's habit of scattering her things all over the house, then Angela needed to decide what she was going to do if Randi persisted with this behavior. Then Angela could sit down with Randi and let her know that she was tired of nagging her and that it didn't seem to be working, so from now on there would be new consequences.

Angela was skeptical, but agreed to try out the approach. She sat Randi down and told her that she'd come up with a new plan. Randi had a choice: She could either pick up her things, Angela said, or Angela would keep her things hostage for three days. Randi argued at first. But by evening, to Angela's astonishment, Randi's belongings had mysteriously disappeared from their usual drop spots on the dining-room table and the living-room floor. Giving Randi a choice kept it from being a battle, and reduced the anger on both sides.

This type of approach will save you from making idle threats like, "If I find your clothes around the house one more time, I'm never going to buy you any new clothes again!," or "If you don't do your homework, you'll be grounded for a month!" When we don't plan ahead, we make idle threats. Our children then test us to see if we are going to follow through.

By choosing one thing to work on at a time, both you and your children will experience more immediate success, and you'll gain greater cooperation as you work to change other inappropriate behavior.

Step 2: Ignore what isn't really important to you. Not every problem calls for an intervention. A lot of situations can simply be ignored because your children will stop the inappropriate behavior on their own as soon as you stop paying attention to it. Suppose your son comes in and takes a handful of cookies, and you say, "You can have two," and he says, "I want three." You have to decide whether it is worth your energy to argue over one cookie. You need to find your own balance between ignoring and intervening.

Ask yourself, "Are my words going to inspire cooperation or precipitate a battle? Would I even bother if this were the neighbor's child instead of mine? Can I really let this one go, or do I need to stand firmly?" These questions will help you to think before you incite a needless riot or set a limit you may regret having to enforce later.

We can safely ignore about 95 percent of the minor misbehaviors that bother us. When I say "minor misbehavior," I mean things like sibling arguments, whining, getting dirty, spilling milk, goofiness, or refusing to eat their vegetables. Frequently children only persevere with a behavior to get a reaction from you. That's why sometimes it's more instructive to ignore behavior you can tolerate, and save your energy for the more important issues.

Step 3: Take time to think before acting or reacting. Children always want the answers to their questions the minute they are asked; consequently we often pressure ourselves to answer our children instantly—to run on "child-time."

Frank, a harried father of thirteen-year-old twin girls, reported to my class one evening how he had learned to cope with his daughters' pressuring him for an instant answer. He established a rule that his daughters had to back off to give him time and physical distance to think after making a request. If they didn't do this, his automatic response would be no. Given these parameters, his kids quickly realized it was in their best interests to cooperate.

When we respond under pressure, we often say things we later regret. How many times have you automatically told your children no, and within seconds realized that, had you thought for a moment, you would have responded differently?

Liza, a single mother with a high-pressure career, is a perfect example of this pattern of action. She had just got home from work and had rushed into the kitchen to start dinner when Jenny came bursting in and began to plead, "Mom, can I spend the night at Alison's tomorrow?" Liza's immediate reaction was no. Jenny persisted, "Why not? It's not a school night—please let me." "I'm busy trying to get dinner ready," Liza snapped back. "I don't want to be bothered now. The answer is no." Jenny ran out, yelling through her tears, "You're so mean! It's not fair!" As Liza finished cooking dinner, she had a quiet moment to think about Jenny's request and realized that there really wasn't a good reason for not letting her daughter spend the night with her friend. Liza was just reacting to the pressure of coming home and feeling rushed, and consequently made a snap judgment. Liza later went into Jenny's room and told her that she'd thought it over, and the sleepover date was fine. Then she went further and informed

Jenny, "When I first get home from work, I feel rushed to change and get dinner started. It's not a good time to ask me important questions."

When we give ourselves time to think, we become less re-active and more effective at discipline. We *can* teach our children not to pressure us.

Step 4: Encourage cooperation. Every action your child takes is his best effort at getting his needs met. This is a hard one to remember in the heat of the moment, but it is invariably true whether his behavior is acceptable or not. When your child is misbehaving, ask yourself these questions: "What need is he expressing through this behavior?" "How can I help my child to get his need met in a more positive way?"

A father described his eight-year-old daughter as bossy, stubborn, and sassy. "Judy always wants her own way. She al-ways has to have the last word, and she talks back." I asked him what need he thought she was expressing through this behavior. He thought for a minute: "I guess she needs to con-trol what's happening to her, to feel powerful." I then asked him, "Is there enough structure and routines in your home to provide Judy with a sense of safety and security?" As we talked further, he began to realize that there was, in fact, a lack of limits and prescribed routines. First we worked on instituting more structure into the daily routines. Then I asked him to look at what positive use these so-called negative qualities might be. Could stubbornness, bossiness, and sassiness have an up-side? "Well," he said, "I suppose you could also describe her as independent, with a strong will and strong opinions."

Every so-called negative trait our children have also has an-other side to it. That's why we need to help our kids to chan-nel their strengths in positive directions. With a child like Judy, who needs control, it helps to allow her to make choices when-ever possible: "Do you want to set the table, or empty the dish-washer?" Reinforce the positive ways in which she uses these qualities: "You are very determined to get what you want. I like that." Recognize how difficult it is for her to accept dis-appointment: "It must have been hard for you to keep playing when you knew you had lost the game." These comments let her know that you recognize her struggles and understand what she is coping with.

A misbehaving child is subconsciously saying, "I want to be loved. I want to belong, and I don't know any better way to do it." A misbehaving child is a discouraged child. She is telling you that she doesn't feel valued or connected, and that she believes that the way to gain significance and belonging is through misbehavior. The best way to help a discouraged child is to use encouragement. Encouragement is to a child what water is to a plant. Children's spirits shrivel up and die without it.

When working to change your children's behavior, think about going for improvement rather than perfection. In other words focus less on the end ideal you wish they would achieve and more on the next step they need to take on their road to that goal. Perfection is such an unrealistic standard that kids feel intimidated. They would rather not try than to be continually faced with failure. When we recognize any improvement, it is encouraging to our kids and inspires their efforts. It also teaches them the lesson that many small steps are the way to eventually achieving a larger goal.

We need to inspire the best in our kids daily, so that they know they can become their best selves. You can always find something to praise about your children's strengths and talents. "It looks like you are putting in a lot of time studying for your English test"; "I appreciate the way you included your sister in your game." "You took a lot of care organizing your toy shelf." Build on these qualities, and your kids will grow and blossom.

THE POWER OF THE POSITIVE

Motivating your children to cooperate is the key to effective discipline. When our relationship with our children is a series of power struggles, we are bound to lose. As we've said before, children, if given half a chance, want to please us and to be positive, contributing family members. But at the same time they are attempting to explore and develop their own individuality. If we are continually trying to enforce our point of view over theirs, they will instinctively resist, and we end up in an ongoing battle of wills. If they win the battle, we will have an out-of-control child. If we win it, we will end up with a child whose individuality has been suppressed or defeated. However, by using encouragement plus incentives for behaving appropriately within the everyday family structure, you build your child's positive self-image and sense of individuality because you are placing the power in his or her hands.

The majority of the time we spend with our children needs to be positive so that it makes them feel good about themselves. One father recently announced in class that his daughter, as he put it, doesn't act stubborn and lazy anymore. When he took the time to express appreciation for her participation rather than scolding her for her shortcomings, he realized that her "stubbornness" and "laziness" had really been a lack of confidence and fear of not doing things well enough to please him. His encouragement and expression of appreciation inspired her to feel more confident about her efforts and thus to help more.

Encouraging our children takes time—quality time. When our kids can count on us to give them focused attention, many problems melt away. The child who needs love the most is frequently the child who is the most difficult to love.

DO YOU STILL LOVE ME?

When we moved to Los Angeles, I was very busy completing my thesis and taking classes. Ama was having a difficult time making the adjustment, and was waking up several times a night crying and complaining of being scared. One day she came into my room and asked if she was still important to me.

After talking with her for a while, I discovered that she was feeling left out, now that so much of my time was devoted to my career. We decided that we would make a date for Thursday afternoons, and that I would pick her up from school and we would do whatever she wanted to do. Some days we went shopping, other days we fed the ducks at the park, sometimes we would go home and play board games together with no distractions. This was a special, nurturing time for both of us, which allowed us to reestablish her specialness despite my busy schedule. And after a few weeks of our Thursday "dates" I noticed that Ama's night fears began to calm. One of the most powerful ways of expressing love to our children is by spending focused time with them. We don't usually think of this as part of discipline, but it is essential. By spending time with our children, we actually inspire their cooperative behavior.

Step 5: Hold a positive expectation. Stop for a minute and ask yourself how you describe your children: responsible, lazy, cooperative, immature, competent? Our children are very sensitive to our attitudes about them. Have you ever noticed that parents who see their children as responsible seem to have responsible children? The mechanism behind this is not mysterious. If you perceive your child as responsible and cooperative, you will, without even being consciously aware of it, give him more opportunities to demonstrate his competence and to develop a sense of responsibility. The more trust and confidence you place in your child, the more your child learns that he is worthy of trust, and the more trustworthy he becomes.

BEING A CHEERLEADER FOR YOUR KIDS

Four-year-old Jerome was refusing to get himself dressed in the morning. "I'm too little," he would insist. "I can't get dressed all by myself. You have to help me do it." Every morning his parents would go through the same routine. Alice, his mother, was especially frustrated, since she had to rush to get her children ready for carpool and get off to work. "You're just a spoiled brat!" she would sometimes say to Jerome in exasperation. "Your sister Becky dresses herself. And there's no reason you couldn't do it too! I don't like you when you give me such a hard time. Grow up!"

When Alice presented her dilemma in one of my classes, I introduced her to the concept of the "star chart." I suggested that she make a chart that had ten to twelve squares on it, like a calendar. I suggested that she write in every third square the word "surprise." I also asked her to enlist Jerome's help in making the chart. I suggested that she take him to the store to pick out some stars to use on the chart. The idea is that every day that he gets dressed by himself he can put a star on his chart. I asked Alice not to leave any square blank. If Jerome missed a day, he should not be penalized, but it would just take him a bit longer to fill in the squares. On the day when he reached the surprise square, he should get a small surprise like a ball or a trip to the park with one of his parents. Because young children need more short-term encouragement than older kids, I had her break the task down into smaller steps so Jerome could feel successful along the way.

Alice went home and told Jerome about her new idea. He got really excited. And that night after dinner, they got out the crayons and sat down at the kitchen table and made the chart. The next day she took him to the store and they bought red, gold, and silver stars. The following morning Alice sent Jerome to his room to get dressed. Jerome came into the kitchen completely dressed, but carrying his shoes and socks. "Jerome, good job getting dressed," Alice remarked, remembering to give him lots of positive feedback. She sat down and helped her son get started with putting his socks on, then added, "I bet that tomorrow you'll be able to get your socks on, too. Go over and put a star on your chart. Good work!" By the end of the week Jerome was dressing himself completely.

Another way for us to show our confidence in our kids is to allow them to assume new responsibilities. Twelve-year-old

Margery wanted to take the bus to her dentist appointment on her own. Her parents were willing to trust Margery's ability to get to her appointment on time. This was Margery's first chance to demonstrate to her parents her growing capacity to be responsible. That night at the dinner table her father asked, "How was your adventure today?" Margery beamed. "I stopped for a snack after school. Then I caught the three-thirty bus and got to my appointment ten minutes early." It was evident that she felt very proud and more confident.

"Children find in the eyes of their parents the mirror in which they define themselves in the relationship," psychologist William Glasser has written. "Fill it with nothing, they become nothing. They have a tremendous ability to live down to the lowest expectation in any environment." We need to consciously train ourselves to hold high, *realistic* expectations for our children. This lets them know that we believe in their capabilities while supporting them in developing and growing into their abilities.

Step 6: Communicate clearly and concisely. Do you ever feel like a broken record, "Clean up this mess! Clean up this mess!" and yet you don't get results? The average parent scolds or nags a preschool age child about fifty-five times a day.[1] No kidding. Those are the actual statistics. Do you realize how much energy all that nagging takes? And worse yet, nagging your children simply doesn't work. Our kids learn to tune us out. Do you talk to your child while she is watching TV and wonder why she doesn't look up when you speak? Or do you find yourself repeating instructions constantly? These are all signs of ineffective communication. Here are some ways to improve your communication skills:

EXPRESS WHAT YOU WANT IN SIMPLE, POSITIVE, SPECIFIC TERMS

Kevin was driving his three-year-old son, Jed, to preschool. He had been having trouble with Jed, who never wanted Kevin to leave when they arrived at school. On this particular day, Kevin tried a new approach. While they were in the car, Kevin turned to Jed: "How about being a big boy today and not crying when we get to school?" Jed looked over at his father, smiled, and chirped, "Okay, Daddy." However, as Jed and Kevin walked in the front door, Jed burst into tears and clung to his father's leg. Kevin had set the stage for a self-fulfilling prophecy by telling his son that what he anticipated would be the usual difficult scene. Asking Jed to be a good boy didn't describe the behavior Kevin wanted. Instead of telling him not to cry, Kevin might have said, "Today, we're going to have a happy good-bye kiss." By stating what we want clearly and in the positive, we let our kids know what it is we want and give them the message that they are capable of doing what we ask of them.

Most of the time we tell our children what we *don't* want them to do rather than what we *do* want: "Don't spill your milk!" "Don't leave your clothes on the floor." "Don't pull the dog's hair." If we state what we want in the positive, our children will have a better idea of how to cooperate and what to do to be successful. Say, "I want you to pick up your toys now" instead of "Stop making such a mess!" Be specific in your requests. Instead of saying, "Be good," say, "I know you can cooperate with your sister while we are out." Express a specific desire with positive expectancy.

DON'T ASK QUESTIONS, GIVE COMMANDS

A mother calls her daughter, Michele. "Time for lunch." She calls her two more times with no response. The neighbor overhears her and says to the little girl who is playing in her yard, "Didn't you hear your mother call you for lunch? Why didn't you go in?" The little girl looked up at the neighbor with a sheepish grin and said, "She hasn't screamed at me yet!"

The language you use to make a request will have a lot of

bearing on its effectiveness. Whenever I counsel parents who are having difficulty getting their children to cooperate, I ask them to examine the specific language they are using. One of the common mistakes I run across is when parents, in an attempt to treat their children respectfully, frame their requests in the form of questions. For example, "Dan, do you want to put your toys away before we go to the park?" instead of "Dan, when you put your toys away, then we can go to the park." Rather than, "Susan, would you like me to help you get out of the bathtub now?" say, "Susan, it's time to get out of the bathtub now," or "Let me help you get out." By asking a question instead of using a polite command, what we are doing is giving our kids choices we don't mean them to have. And then we further confuse them by becoming upset when they answer honestly, "no." When that same request is phrased as a polite command, it is far more effective. To avoid confusion, make a statement: "Time to eat lunch now," or "Let's brush our teeth."

Deborah and Timmy were shopping at the mall. They had stopped in the pet store to look at the puppies. Deborah said to Timmy, "Do you want to go and buy your jacket now?" Timmy, who was totally absorbed watching the puppies crawl all over each other said, "No, Mommy. Not now. I want to stay and watch more." When Deborah realized that she had got herself into a bind, she revised her approach and said, "Tim, when the big hand gets to the five on the clock, we have to leave to do our errands. That's five more minutes." When the time came, Deborah spoke clearly and firmly. "It's time to go now." And Timmy went. Only ask a question if you are willing to accept "no" for an answer.

Step 7: Give your children choices. There are times when polite commands are appropriate, and there are many other times when the best way to engage a child's cooperation is to offer a choice. For lots of parents the idea of giving your children choices is foreign. When I presented the concept in one of my seminars, a father stood up and protested. "Doesn't giving our kids choices mean that we are giving in and showing weakness?" Actually quite the opposite is true. When we offer our children the opportunity to make choices, we teach them to think clearly. We show our strength as well as our flexibility in considering their needs and concerns. By giving our kids choices, we help them to learn about responsibility and prepare them for greater independence.

However, it should be noted that there are two kinds of choices—*unlimited* and *limited*. When you give your child an unlimited choice, he can come up with anything. For example, "Where do you want to go for dinner?" He can say, "To the moon," and you may not be willing to go there. A limited choice would be, "Do you want to go to eat pizza or hamburgers?"

Limiting choices defuses the power struggle that can develop between parents and kids. You can offer your children limited choices such as, "Do you want cereal or an egg for breakfast?," or "Do you want to wear your red shirt or your plaid one?" "Do you want to wash the dishes before or after your TV show?" Offer them a choice within a structure, and you will be happy with whatever they choose. Only offer unlimited choices when you would honestly be content no matter what they pick. Frequently we give our children choices, and then we resent them or get angry with them for their decision.

Rosemary asked her daughter, Heather, "What do you want to do as a special treat?" Heather immediately replied, "I want to go to the amusement park and take a friend." Rosemary wasn't prepared for this elaborate a trip. She said, "We were just there. I don't want to spend all day there again!" Heather got very quiet, muttered under her breath, "You lied to me," and wouldn't talk to her mother for quite a while. Rosemary, of course, felt guilty, and didn't know how to make it up to Heather. If she had offered her a limited choice, both Rosemary and Heather would have been happier. For example, "Do you want to go to the park, to the movies, or to the children's museum for your special treat?" Limit your children's choices toward alternatives that fit with your time, energy, and budget.

DISCIPLINE WITH LOVE: A PRACTICAL GUIDE

Step 8: Speak assertively. Ama came into my room one day and asked if she could go out with her friends. I said no, in a very noncommittal way. A few minutes later she was back and asked me, "Why?" Then she got on her soapbox. "It's not fair!" she pleaded in eloquent, martyrlike tones. "Please can I go out with my friends?" "Let me think about it," I replied. Again came the plea. I finally got so tired of listening to her that I gave in and yelled, "Yes, go ahead!"

When we set limits, our tone of voice and attitude should convey strength of purpose. We must be confident, firm, and reassuring. When we are wishy-washy, or screaming out of control, it's hard for our children to believe that we are sane and sincere. The louder we yell, the less effective we are. We need to sound confident and calm and let our attitude communicate that we expect them to listen to us.

When we use direct, assertive messages, we leave no doubt in our children's minds as to what we want them to do. "I want you to put your toys away now." "It's time to do your homework." "It's bedtime now. Off you go."

To emphasize your point, make eye contact with your children when speaking to them. Let's say you walk into the living room and your son has all of his Teenage Mutant Ninja Turtles and GI Joe figures spread out for the final battle. "Teddy," you tell him, "why don't you start putting your toys away? It's almost lunchtime." "I don't want to," Teddy replies. "I hate cleaning up!" At this point you need to walk over to him, look him in the eye, and say, "I know you don't like to clean up, but it's time to put your toys away now!"

Step 9: Be consistent. When I ask kids why they don't listen to their parents, inevitably they say, "Because they don't really mean what they say. They'll tell me something, and then either forget or don't make me do it, so why should I take them seriously?"

Consistency means we are willing to back up our words with actions. We need to learn to talk less and act more. When you want to change your children's behavior, you have to make it a priority. If you've told your daughter that you would leave the restaurant if she continued to whine and cry, you can't wait until you finish eating before you make good on your promise. You have to leave the restaurant. Then let your daughter know that you won't be taking her out to eat again until you have some indication that she can behave herself. Although it may be a big inconvenience, it will accomplish your goal of changing your child's behavior. You'll have an easier time when you realize that it's your consistent actions more than your words that teach your children you mean business.

Will kids test the limits to find out how firm they are? You can count on it. But if you're consistent in enforcing the limits, your children will learn to respect both the limits and you as well. When you keep the boundary fixed, after a while your children will stop trying to move it.

If you establish behavioral rules, you won't have to deal with continual crises. One mother told me that she had posted the house rules in the kitchen. This allowed her daughters to gear their behavior to their parents' expectations. Some of the things she included were: no hitting, no running in the house, put toys away after you and your guests play with them. You can make two sets of rules with your kids, personal rules and house rules. Personal rules would be: Brush your teeth before bed, shower every day, make your bed. House rules are more along the lines of things that affect your family as a whole: no ball playing or running in the house, no hitting, and be on time for meals. Once you establish rules, determine consequences, and follow through, your children will stop testing your limits. They will learn that it's a waste of time.

There's a story about a hungry caged mouse. A piece of cheese was dropped into the cage several times, and the mouse scurried to eat it. Then a clear glass divider was placed into the cage, which kept the mouse from reaching the side where the food had been placed. Several more pieces of food were put into the divided section, only this time the mouse could only throw itself against the glass. Finally the pain caused the mouse to give up. After the glass divider was removed, the mouse didn't try to get the food. Experience had taught the mouse that the attempt would result in worthless pain.

A limit for your kids is a lot like the glass divider. If it's there long enough, our kids get tired of running into it. They eventually stop testing our resolve and accept that the limit exists, even if we are not actively enforcing it.

Acting consistently also means enforcing the consequence without making your children feel bad. The paradox is that when we become more consistent without getting mad, yelling, or compromising, discipline becomes easier. Our kids know what our emotional limits are, and they will push us to them. Stay firm with what you say and follow through with what you promise, and in the long run your children will cooperate, with fewer power struggles along the way.

Step 10: Use natural or logical consequences. One effective way to help children learn without engendering anger or resentment is to use consequences. Consequences avoid a power struggle because they spring naturally from the situation.

There are two types of consequences: natural and logical. Natural consequences arise from the situation. Logical consequences require an adult to intervene to help the child experience the effects of his misbehavior. First, natural consequences:

Ross forgets his coat, and he gets cold. Carmen leaves her wet towel on the floor, and when she needs it again, it's still wet. Tim forgets his homework, and gets lower marks at school. Jake doesn't eat lunch, and gets hungry during math. Gloria dawdles in the morning, and receives a tardy slip. These are consequences the environment enforces. They occur without the intervention of an adult.

Ten-year-old Aaron was constantly being nagged by his mother to pick up his dirty Little League uniform and to put it in the laundry basket. Aaron, like most kids, didn't respond to nagging. He did, however, continually complain to his mother about not having a clean uniform to wear. Sue would often do a quick load of laundry when Aaron didn't have a clean uniform and complained loudly enough.

Sue decided to try using natural consequences. She told

Aaron, "I know you can put your uniform in the hamper if you want it washed. It's up to you to do so, otherwise it will stay dirty."

Aaron, not taking his mother seriously, left his dirty uniform on the floor, and then complained when he had nothing clean to wear to Little League practice. "I bet you want me to do an emergency wash for you," his mother responded. "Well, I know you can come up with another solution to your problem." Then Sue went into the bedroom to avoid further discussion. Aaron was angry and upset that he had to wear a dirty uniform. But he learned that his mother meant what she said. Aaron now remembers to put his dirty uniform in the laundry basket because he now knows that this is the only way that it will get clean.

It's hard to allow consequences to occur when your children are upset by them. Nevertheless, you have to show them that you mean what you say. In many cases the most effective thing you can do is to *do nothing*. This can be more difficult than punishing your children. If your teenage son doesn't give his sister a birthday present, she'll feel upset. If your daughter forgets her soccer gear, she'll have to sit out the game.

It may not always be possible, however, to use natural consequences. There are three instances when you would instead choose to use logical consequences. The first is the most obvious, when your child's safety is at stake; second, when the natural consequences interfere with another's rights; and finally when the result of the behavior doesn't appear to bother the child. Let me explain:

If your child's safety is at stake, that obviously becomes your first priority. For example, your child is playing in the front yard unsupervised, and he runs out near the street—using natural consequences to teach responsibility here is out of the question. Instead, you impose logical consequences and limit his play to either the backyard or to inside the house until he can learn not to run near the street.

Second, we must resort to logical consequences when the natural consequences interfere with other people's rights or well-being. We can't allow our children to hit another person, for instance. A logical consequence of one child trying to hit another is that the instigator not be allowed to play until she has cooled off. Keep in mind that the point of isolation isn't to punish your child or to make her suffer, but to change her behavior.

Finally, when the result of the behavior doesn't appear to bother the child, then natural consequences are ineffective.[2]

Four-year-old Jesse attends preschool, and his mother, Paula, came into one parenting class at her wit's end. She had been fighting with Jesse to get him dressed in the mornings. Paula and her husband both worked and had a tight morning schedule. Paula had taught Jesse how to dress himself when he was two. They had bought clothes that would be easy for him to manage. Paula had also gotten into the habit of laying out his clothes for him the night before to ease the morning rush. The arrangement was that Jesse was to get up and dress himself, come in and have breakfast with his parents, and if there was time before leaving for school, he could watch morning cartoons.

This worked fine until one morning Jesse dawdled until it was time to leave. His parents had to help him dress; he was late to school, and they were late to work. Soon a new pattern developed of dawdling and tardiness to preschool. After reasoning with him and nagging him for weeks to no avail, Paula was at the breaking point. Obviously Jesse didn't care in the least that he was late, so natural consequences were useless in this situation. However, with the guidance of the class, the next morning Paula got Jesse up and told him, "You can either get dressed at home right now or you can dress when we get to school. You decide." Jesse looked at his mother in disbelief. Then Paula gathered up his clothes and carried them out to the car. He cried all the way to school, but Paula ignored it. When Jesse arrived at school, the teacher said, "I see you didn't get dressed this morning. Take your clothes into the bathroom and come out as soon as you're dressed."

From that morning on Jesse was always dressed and ready

to go. On the rare morning when he would dawdle, his mother or father would remind him, "It looks like you're deciding to get dressed at school today." Jesse would hurry and finish dressing. This use of logical consequences allowed the child to make a choice and to live with the consequences of that choice. There was no need for screaming, nagging, or punishment. Some children don't care if they have a clean room, brush their teeth, wash their face, bathe, or don't do their homework. When this is the case, it's useful to switch to logical consequences to help your children learn responsible behavior.

CONSEQUENCES VS. PUNISHMENT

Parents ask, "What is the difference between punishment and consequences?" Punishment is directed *at* the child. To punish, says the *Oxford English Dictionary of Etymology,* is to "cause to suffer for an offense." Punishment will never accomplish your purpose. It may establish temporary external controls for your child's behavior, but it doesn't encourage the development of self-discipline. The underlying message in punishment is, "You either do what I say, or else you'll pay." When you offer your children choices and use consequences, you encourage your children to make responsible decisions and to bear the results of their actions.

Here are a few examples to illustrate the difference between consequences and punishment: 1) "Mom and I are trying to sleep. Either turn down the TV or go play outside. It's up to you" instead of "Bonnie, turn off the TV or I'll yank the cord out of the wall." 2) "Claude, Lucy is coming to clean today. You can either pick up your toys or I will collect them and put them away for the week. You decide" instead of, "Danny, how many times have I told you to put your toys away? I can't possibly clean with your room in such a mess. No TV today."

Here is a formula psychologist and author Rudolph Dreikurs

DISCIPLINE WITH LOVE: A PRACTICAL GUIDE

described in his book *A New Approach to Discipline* to differentiate punishment from logical consequences. The formula is called the three R's: related, reasonable, and respectful.[3] If any of the three R's are missing, your action is not a logical consequence. When a child tracks dirt into the house, what is the related consequence? Have him vacuum up the dirt. It would be disrespectful to him to say, "What a slob! How can you be such a pig?" If your child doesn't know what to do because you haven't taken the time to teach him, this is an opportunity to teach him a new skill. Mistakes are wonderful opportunities for learning.

Many parents evoke resentment, rebellion, or bad feelings by imposing unreasonable consequences on their children: "If you talk back to me one more time, you're grounded for a month." "If you don't get your homework done, no TV for a week." "You tease your sister one more time, and you won't come to the family picnic." "You were late coming home. No telephone for a week." These consequences are really punishments, because the parental attitude is one of retaliation: "I want to make you feel sorry for what you've done, and to show you who's boss."

When you choose a consequence, it shouldn't be overwhelming. It should be related to the behavior so that your children can avoid the consequence the next time. And it should be carried out in a matter-of-fact, respectful manner. We don't have to invent difficulties. We simply have to think of the natural or logical consequences and use them despite the fact that they may cause discomfort and inconvenience.

It's normal to get annoyed and angry with our children, but using force and anger isn't going to accomplish our goal of teaching our kids. Parents often turn consequences into punishment by using an angry tone of voice, or by not connecting the consequences with the behavior that caused it. Consequences should be given respectfully, they should be related to the behavior, and they should be reasonable.

WHEN/THEN

One way to teach our children to be responsible is through the concept of when/then: "When you have emptied the dishwasher, then you may go out and play." We can start teaching our children this as early as they can walk. "When you pick up your toys, then I'll read you a story." This concept can apply to all areas of your children's lives. "When you have cleaned your room, then you may watch TV." Or, "When you have finished brushing your teeth, then we will play a game." This concept helps children learn to be accountable and responsible for what they want. We need to teach our kids that privileges go hand in hand with responsibility.

The goal in using both natural and logical consequences is to give the responsibility for the way your children behave back to them. When we nag our children about their annoying behavior, they don't have to change because we have assumed responsibility for it.

Parents have reported to me that they have trouble following through with consequences because they feel intimidated by their children's reaction. They say they don't want their children to hate them or to be angry with them. When we allow fear of our children's feelings to control our actions, we let them down on a level that is very crucial to their maturation. Discipline is a two-way street: if we want our children to act responsibly, then we have to accept the responsibility for disciplining them. In other words, we ourselves need to be self-disciplined. If we aren't, the natural consequences of our inaction will be our unhappy, insecure, insensitive children and our own stress-filled lives.

Step 11: Discuss the issue calmly. The time to teach your children isn't in the heat of the battle. If your child just broke a glass, it's the least advantageous time to talk to her about improvement. In that moment she is feeling awful, and if you yell at her, she'll just feel more humiliated. She can't learn anything at this time, because she's too busy defending herself. Talk with your child either at bedtime or after enough time has passed to let the emotions settle. You will both have a better perspective on the situation, and your child will be more receptive to the lessons she can learn.

Sometimes it is we who are too upset to deal with the situation effectively. When this happens, we need to find a way to cool down. We can go out for a run, go for a walk, or leave the room. A mother in one of my classes reported that she decided to try an idea that I had suggested in the previous session. At the time she thought it sounded ridiculous. "I was really skeptical," she said, "but when I was on the verge of smacking my son, I took several deep breaths and walked out of the room, and avoided a major battle. I was really surprised at how such a simple technique could work so well." The idea is that when we are upset, it is impossible to think clearly or act sanely. We need to do something to break the energy between our kids and us. The image I like to use is, I imagine that an electrical wire is connecting my daughter and me. If I unplug my end of the cord, the juice stops flowing. It is much easier to solve problems or to discuss the past upsetting situation once we are on the other side of it. Timing is everything.

After we had discussed this issue in class the following week, Robin reported that her daughter had ruined her new lipstick. When she came home, Robin said to Adrienne, "I'm too angry at you right now to talk—you had better stay clear of me." Adrienne left her mother alone. The next morning while driving to school, Robin brought up the subject of the lipstick. "I really was angry that you used my makeup without asking me. I've told you before that I didn't want you playing with my things. What do you think we can do so that it doesn't happen again?" Adrienne thought a minute, then replied, "I'm sorry, Mom, I won't do it again. Can I buy my own pretend makeup to play with? Then I won't want to use yours." Because Robin took time to discuss the incident with her daughter when they were both calm, the discussion was reasonable and productive. She used it as an opportunity to express her feelings to her daughter as well as to think about how they might prevent any further problems from occurring.

Step 12: Forgive and forget. Once the deed is done and the consequence is carried out, it's time to let it go. Many parents lose sight of the fact that our kids are more important to us than anything they could ever do. Sometimes we focus so much on the deed that we forget the critical distinction between our children and their behavior.

The final thing you do after disciplining your children is to put your arms around them and give them a hug and tell them that you love them. No matter what they've done, that hug and reassurance of your love is the most important thing. It says, "I don't approve of your behavior, and these are the consequences, but I love you." Your unconditional love for your kids is central to their feeling secure, lovable, and capable.

When children are involved in more serious incidents, such as drug abuse, stealing, or cheating, they need to know that you are behind them with your love, support, and commitment to help them to change their self-destructive behavior. This doesn't mean that you excuse or ignore the problem, but change occurs more easily and rapidly from a foundation of love and forgiveness.

In my counseling practice, when I've told teens that I need to call their parents, they often plead with me not to call. I don't ever want my child to feel that when she is in trouble she can't talk to me because she is afraid of my reaction. I don't want her to think that I just love her when she's doing well and getting good grades; I want her to know that no matter what she does, she can always come to me and I will be there to love and support her.

Part of parenting is helping your children navigate through the rough seas of life. When they make mistakes, the first person they should come to is you. You don't want to be the one they avoid for fear you'll love them less. Give your kids the message that even when they act inappropriately, you will never change how much you love them.

I'd like to end this chapter by sharing a poem with you that I've always felt sums up the challenge of disciplining your children with love:

> I loved you enough to ask where you were going, with whom, and what time you would be home.
>
> I loved you enough to be silent and let you discover that your new best friend was a creep.
>
> I loved you enough to stand over you for two hours while you cleaned your room. A job that would have taken me fifteen minutes.
>
> I loved you enough to let you assume responsibility for your actions even when the penalties were so harsh they almost broke my heart.
>
> But most of all, I loved you enough to say "no" when I knew you would hate me for it.
>
> Those were the most difficult battles of them all. I'm glad I won them, because in the end you won something, too.
>
> Anonymous

Chapter 10
THE LOVING FAMILY: MAKING IT WORK

"A journey of 1,000 miles must begin with a single step."
—Lao Tzu

One evening as I was rushing out of the house to teach one of my seminars, my daughter was bugging me about whether she could have a friend spend the night. As I frantically threw my notes into my briefcase, I flew into a rage and began yelling at her, "Be quiet, Ama! Can't you see I'm late? I don't have time to talk about this now!"

"I bet you don't teach the parents in your class to do that," she shouted back in a voice loaded with righteous indignation. "Do you tell them how you yell at *me*?" I walked out to my car with my self-image bruised. Here I was teaching this stuff to other parents, and once again I'd lost it.

I gave myself a pep talk as I drove to my class, and reminded myself that I'd have another opportunity to practice my skills. I could count on getting a second chance, probably sooner than I wanted one. I reassured myself that there was no point in beating myself up for yet another transgression. I forgave myself privately and publicly confessed my humanness to my class.

You have a choice. You can take all the information I have shared with you and use it to beat yourself up for the things you've done wrong with your kids. However, what I hope you'll do is take this opportunity to examine your present situation with your children and use the material to make any changes that will improve the quality of your relationships.

This book isn't meant as a magic formula that you blindly follow, but rather offers a series of suggestions that are meant for you to experiment with. Everything I have suggested has been "kitchen tested," both by myself and by hundreds of other parents. You know best what suits your needs, your parenting style, and your child. Experiment, pick-and-choose the approaches that work for you.

THE COURAGE TO BE HUMAN

Like any new skill, the fine art of parenting takes time to integrate and perfect. Think back on the first time you drove a car or learned how to play an instrument. The first time you played a piano, there was probably no recognizable melody. As you continued to practice and study, your skills improved, and you began playing pieces by memory. This is also true with using positive, more effective approaches to parenting.

As you read this book you will continue to learn new skills for understanding and relating more effectively with your family members. You will be trying out different ways of communicating and relating with your children. It is common knowledge that human beings are imperfect and subject to making mistakes. Yet though we all know this, we still have a terrible time accepting it. Most of us continue to demand perfection from ourselves and doom ourselves to terminal frustration and failure. We can be a nurturing parent, an encouraging parent, but it is impossible to be a perfect parent. The most we can expect of ourselves is that we do our best, knowing that there will always be room for improvement.

Please let yourself be imperfect. Most of us hate to make

mistakes, but learning is a process of trial and error. I guarantee that if you don't do something right the first time with your children, you will have another opportunity to refine your skills very soon. Just as I have reminded you to be supportive of your children as they learn and grow, I ask that you be gentle with yourself as well.

Imagine for a moment how wonderful it would be to hear a parent say to their child, "You made a mistake. How wonderful! Let's celebrate the fact that you had the courage to risk learning something new. Now what can you learn from this experience?" We can take every mistake as an opportunity to strengthen our compassion and to model for our children that imperfection simply comes with the territory of being human.

One of my basic beliefs is that parents are always doing the best they can with the information that they have. I have never met a parent who intentionally tried to mess up his or her kids. Most likely everything you've been doing so far is your best effort at raising your children. Any lack you may recognize in your parenting is more likely due to a lack of training than a lack of caring and good intentions.

The wonderful thing about raising children is that it's never too late to learn new skills and improve our relationship with our kids. Each day offers us new opportunities to improve our parenting. We can each change what is required if we start with where we are now and build on that foundation. We need to give ourselves permission to be novices in this challenging job of raising our children. When we allow ourselves to begin from where we presently stand, then all of a sudden our families become wonderful places to learn and practice.

BREAKING THE FAMILY CHAIN

I've got good news and bad news. The bad news is that so much of what we say and do with our children unconsciously echoes our own parents. The good news is that the tools and techniques you have learned here will not only change your own habitual responses, but will also alter age-old family patterns.

"I want things to be different with my kids," a father in one of my seminars admitted. "I felt like a second-class citizen the way my parents denied my feelings, and criticized me all the time. I know that they were doing the best they could, but I want my kids to have it better. Wouldn't it be great if when they're all grown they'd *want* to spend time with me, not just because they'd feel guilty if they didn't?"

With motivation, practice, and patience, you can break the generational shackles that have prevented you from having a fully loving, nurturing family. You can build a relationship with your children based on mutual respect and honest, open communication.

MODELING

Our children's most powerful mode of learning is by imitation. How you are with your children is the most powerful teaching tool you have. The old adage "Do as I say, not as I do" is really not very realistic. No matter what we tell our children, our kids watch what we do more than they listen to what we say.

How do you think you'd feel if you walked into a dentist's office, sat down in the chair, and as your dentist started to lecture you about the virtues of regular brushing and flossing, you noticed that his two front teeth were missing? Or what if you walked in to see your doctor for a cholesterol check and while he's holding forth about how cholesterol is a major factor in heart disease, he is eating a triple-decker pastrami sandwich that's dripping with mayonnaise? You wouldn't exactly be overly eager to take either guy's advice or instruction, would you? (Chances are you'd want to run shrieking out of their offices.)

The same principle applies to parenting. We model for our children on a daily basis. We can't really teach our kids anything through trying to impose our will on them. Even if they acquiesce on the surface, they will rebel internally, and the lesson will have been lost.

When we use more respectful, effective ways of communicating with our kids, we also give them new models for communication with their friends, teachers, and us.

I overheard a telephone conversation between my daughter and a friend in which she said, "I feel angry when you make plans with me and change your mind at the last minute. I feel like you think of me as a standby. If nothing better is happening, you'll do something with me." I was stunned by her honesty and directness. Could she have learned this from me?

Several days later Ama and I were in the car, and I said, "I really don't want to go to the opera with Guy, but I don't want to hurt his feelings." She looked at me. "Mom," she said, "just tell him the truth. You're not doing anyone a favor by feeling one way and acting another." I was stunned by her clarity. She was feeding the lessons I had taught her right *back* to me at a moment when *I* needed to hear them.

OUR CHILDREN ARE OUR GREATEST TEACHERS

One of the gifts we receive from being a parent is that we have another opportunity to relive our own childhoods. Our children bring us a great opportunity for healing. By loving and caring for our kids through the different stages of growth, we have a wonderful opportunity to heal our own inner child.

All of us have hurt and confusion left over from our own childhoods that still affect us as adults. If we are alert to this fact, the mere process of parenting and observing our children can go a long way toward resolving these past hurts. Parenting also gives us the chance to recapture some of the delight of childhood as we share in the joy, excitement, and enthusiasm of our children.

LIGHTENING UP

There is one parenting technique that didn't quite fit into any of the previous chapters but that I guarantee is an essential key to hanging on to your sanity, and that is maintaining a sense of humor. Often we think a situation is much more serious than it really is. Humor can help to defuse negative emotions and potentially explosive situations. (However, we should never, never use humor at our children's expense.) Looking on the light side of a potential conflict can bring a new perspective and often alleviate tension.

There are days when Ama wakes up so grumpy and so disagreeable that it is unpleasant to be around her (that's putting it kindly!). In the past I'd yell at her, trying to convince her to change her attitude, which inevitably made matters worse. One day I decided to make a joke of the situation. She was sitting at the breakfast table spewing forth a steady stream of complaints: "My hair just doesn't look right. I have nothing to wear. There's never anything good to eat in this house. I hate school." And so forth. Instead of my usual reaction of yelling at her to change her rotten attitude, which simply fuels the already raging fire, I said, "Okay, who are you, and what have you done with the *real* Ama? I know you're her evil twin, Cruella. Now, bring back my daughter!" She looked at me as if I were nuts, but within moments we both burst out laughing. The tension was broken, the air was cleared, and we both felt better.

When we can laugh at our own mistakes or at a tense situation, it takes some of the stress out of parenting. Raising children with high self-esteem won't be easy and it won't be painless, but if we can laugh at ourselves, the journey will be a lot easier.

THE LONE RANGER SYNDROME

You can't imagine how many times clients have forlornly described their struggles with their children as if they were the only person in the world who wasn't doing it "right." As I reassured them that there were one or two zillion other parents who had trouble getting their three-year-old to go to bed at night or struggled with getting their kids dressed in the morning, they would look at me in amazement and breathe a grateful sigh of relief.

We are very much like the woman who frantically called her best friend and pleaded with her to come over: "Georgia, you know the new dress I bought when we went shopping last week? Would you mind telling me how great it looks one more time? I'm feeling insecure, and I need to be reminded that it really looks good." That's often how it is with us. We feel overwhelmed and discouraged, and we simply need to be reminded and reassured of the things we inherently know to be true about ourselves and our kids.

Parents need a supportive community, a network of people they can turn to for advice, support, and to share ideas. We weren't meant to raise our children in isolation. We need other parents with whom we can discuss our challenges as well as our joys.

If you aren't already involved in a parents' support group, explore what's available in your community. A parents' support group can be anything from a Mommy and Me class to an offshoot of the PTA to an informal network of good friends. Call your local church or synagogue, ask at your children's school, contact the YWCA or your local Department of Parks and Recreation. If nothing is available in your area, you can start your own group by making a simple flyer and inviting some parents over for an informal talk. If we were meant to know everything and be totally independent, there would only be one of us on the planet. Obviously that isn't the way it's meant to be.

HOPE FOR THE FUTURE

My dream is to help make families a secure place where children and adults can feel enough love that they can turn their attention outward. A child who is emotionally deprived becomes an adult who is always anxiously trying to get her own needs met. But our planet is in a period of crisis. We need a world that is as thoughtful and attentive to human beings as it is to technology and monetary worth.

Too many people have turned their backs on their dreams and have resigned themselves to an attitude of "What difference does it make? I can't really do anything." I don't believe we can afford to have this kind of complacent attitude. The choices you make *do* make a difference. Each one of us *does* count. The adults of today stand on the shoulders of the people we learned to be as children. Childhood is a time when the foundations for life are laid by our parents. So today holds the key to the future.

Creating peace in the world starts with creating peace in our families. It's up to us to provide the richest environment possible so that our children can grow up to express their fullest humanity. What more rewarding responsibility could you have than to raise a generation of loving, compassionate, responsible, caring, productive adults? When I think about the possibility of a world filled with this sort of nurturing individual, I am filled with hope and awe.

And there are other rewards. . . .

Ama and I were driving home from the movies. We were talking about the film we had just seen, singing old James Taylor songs, and thoroughly enjoying ourselves. Ama glanced over at me and said, "Mom, I'm really glad you're my mother. I sometimes feel so bad for my friends when I hear them complain about how their parents treat them—I don't think a lot of parents really respect their kids as people. You know what I mean? Like my friend Jodie, whose mother ripped up all her pictures of her friend just because she was mad about something Jodie did. I feel like no matter what happens, you're really there for me, and that who I am is really okay with you."

I felt the tears well up in my eyes and got a lump in my throat. A moment like this makes all my doubts fade away and makes the years of hard work and sacrifice all worthwhile.

NOTES

Chapter 1: The Best Gift You Can Give Your Children

1. *HHS News* (Washington, D.C.: U.S. Department of Health & Human Services, 1988).
2. *Los Angeles Times*, May 15, 1989.
3. H. Clemes and R. Bean, *Self-Esteem: The Key To Your Child's Well-Being* (New York: G. P. Putnam's Sons, 1981).
4. Ibid.
5. V. Satir, *Making Contact* (Millbrea: Celestial Arts, 1976).
6. Adapted from Clemes and Bean, op. cit.

Chapter 2: Parents Have Needs, Too!

1. U.S. Census Bureau March 1988 report.
2. V. Satir, story told at Process Community VI, Crested Butte, Colorado, July 1986.
3. C. Gilligan, *In a Different Voice: Psychological Theory and Women's Development* (Cambridge: Harvard University Press, 1982).
4. D. W. Winnicott, "Transitional Objects & Transitional Phenomena," *Collected Papers* (London: Tavistock, 1958).
5. Adapted from A. Saunders and B. Remsberg, *The Stress-Proof Child: A Loving Parent's Guide* (New York: Holt, Rinehart and Winston, 1984).
6. J. Campbell, *The Power of Myth* (Garden City, N.Y.: Doubleday, 1988).

Chapter 3: Falling in Love with Your Kids

1. S. M. Peck, *The Road Less Traveled: A New Psychology of Love, Traditional Values and Spiritual Growth* (New York, Simon & Schuster, 1978).
2. National Random Sample done of 600 adults by the University of Michigan Institute of Social Research, cited in *U.S. News & World Report*, October 27, 1986.
3. L. Albert and M. Popkin, *Quality Parenting* (New York: Ballantine Books, 1987).

4. R. A. Spitz, "Anaclitic Depression," *Journal of Psychoanalytic Study of the Child*, Vol. 2 (1946).
5. Study done by psychologist Janice Gibson and her colleagues at the University of Pittsburgh and cited in *Psychology Today*, March 1988.
6. L. Buscaglia, *Living, Loving and Learning* (New York: Holt, Rinehart and Winston, 1982).
7. Study cited by W. Dyer, *What Do We Really Want for Our Children?* (New York: William Morrow & Co., 1985).
8. G. Jampolsky, *Teach Only Love* (New York: Bantam Books, 1983).
9. M. L. Jacobsen, *How to Keep Your Family Together and Still Have Fun* (Grand Rapids, MI: Zondervan, 1969).
10. Antoine de Saint-Exupéry, *The Little Prince* (New York: Harcourt Brace Jovanovich, 1971).

Chapter 4: The Magic of Encouragement

1. D. Dinkmeyer and R. Dreikurs, *Encouraging Children to Learn: The Encouragement Process* (Englewood Cliffs, N.J.: Prentice Hall, 1963).
2. A study conducted at the University of Calgary, cited in *Parents Magazine*, March 1989.
3. A study cited by Jack Canfield, conducted at the University of Iowa.
4. Adapted from a story heard in a lecture given by Michael Popkin, Ph.D., in Los Angeles, 1987. See also M. Popkin, *Active Parenting* (San Francisco: Harper & Row, 1987).
5. H. Ginott, *Between Parent and Child* (New York: Avon, 1961).
6. N. Samalin, *Loving Your Child Is Not Enough: Positive Discipline That Works* (New York: Viking, 1987).
7. Lee Canter, *Assertive Discipline for Parents* (Santa Monica, Calif.: Canter and Associates, 1982).
8. R. Rosenthal and L. Jacobson, *Pygmalion in the Classroom* (New York: Holt, Rinehart and Winston, 1968).
9. A study cited by S. Isaacs, *Who's in Control? A Parent's Guide to Discipline* (New York: Perigee Books, 1986).
10. J. Canfield, *Self-Esteem in the Classroom* (Pacific Palisades, Calif.: Self-Esteem Seminars, 1986).
11. Z. Ziglar, *Raising Positive Kids in a Negative World* (Nashville, Tenn.: Thomas Nelson Inc., 1985).

Chapter 5: Helping Children with Feelings

1. M. McKay and P. Fanning, *Self-Esteem: A Proven Program of Cognitive Techniques for Assessing, Improving and Maintaining Your Self-Esteem* (Oakland, Calif.: New Harbinger, 1987).

2. Adapted from the works of C. Rogers, *Client-Centered Therapy: Its Current Practice, Implications and Theory* (Boston: Houghton Mifflin, 1951); H. Ginott, *Between Parent and Child* (New York: Avon, 1956); T. Gordon, *P.E.T. in Action* (New York: Putnam Sons, 1976); A. Faber and E. Mazlish, *How to Talk So Kids Will Listen and Listen So Kids Will Talk* (New York: Avon, 1980).

3. Ginott, op. cit.

4. Adapted from Faber and Mazlish, op. cit., and M. Popkin, *Active Parenting* (Atlanta: Active Parenting Inc., 1983).

5. Adapted from A. Saunders and B. Remsberg, *The Stress-Proof Child: A Loving Parent's Guide* (New York: Holt, Rinehart and Winston, 1984).

Chapter 6: Anger in the Family

1. T. Gordon, *Parent Effectiveness Training: P.E.T.* (New York: Peter H. Wyden, 1970).

2. Research done by Albert Merhabian as cited in *Messages: The Communication Skills Book* (Oakland, CA: New Harbinger Publications, 1983).

3. Adapted from the Love Letter Process developed by John Gray, Ph.D., in his book *What You Feel You Can Heal* (Mill Valley, Calif.: Heart Publishing, 1984) and in the book *How to Make Love All the Time*, by Barbara De Angelis, Ph.D. (New York: Dell, 1987).

Chapter 7: Raising Responsible Kids

1. Adapted from M. Popkin, *Active Parenting* (Atlanta: Active Parenting, 1983).

2. Adapted from W. Dyer, *Choosing Your Own Greatness*, an audiocassette program (Chicago: Nightingale Conant, 1987).

Chapter 8: Facing the *D* Word

1. Dr. Irwin Hyman, director of Temple University's National Center for the Study of Corporal Punishment and Alternatives in the Schools, cites a Harris Poll released in the summer 1989.

Chapter 9: Discipline with Love: A Practical Guide

1. Statistics cited in J. Allen, *What Do I Do When?* (San Luis Obispo, Calif.: Impact Publishers, 1983).

2. J. Nelsen, *Positive Discipline* (Fair Oaks, Calif.: Sunrise Press, 1981).

3. R. Dreikurs and L. Grey, *A New Approach to Discipline: Logical Consequences* (New York: Hawthorn Books, 1968).

SUGGESTED READING LIST

Bettelheim, B. *A Good Enough Parent: A Book on Child-Rearing*. New York: Alfred A. Knopf, 1987.

Brazelton, T. B. *Toddlers and Parents*. New York: Delacorte, 1969.

—— *Working and Caring*. Menlo Park: Addison-Wesley, 1987.

Briggs, D. C. *Your Child's Self-Esteem*. Garden City, N.Y.: Doubleday, 1970.

Clarke, J. I. *Self-Esteem: A Family Affair*. Minneapolis, MN: Winston Press, 1978.

Clarke, J. I, and C. Dawson. *Growing Up Again*. Center City, MN: Hazelden, 1989.

Crary, E. *Kids Can Cooperate: A Practical Guide to Teaching Problem Solving*. Seattle: Parenting Press, 1984.

Dinkmeyer, D., and G. McKay. *Raising a Responsible Child*. New York: Simon & Schuster, 1973.

—— *The Parent's Handbook: Systematic Training for Effective Parenting (STEP)*. Circle Pines, MN: American Guidance Services, 1982.

Dreikurs, R., and V. Soltz. *Children: The Challenge*. New York: E. P. Dutton, 1964.

Dyer, W. W. *What Do You Really Want for Your Children?* New York: William Morrow & Company, 1985.

Elkind, D. *The Hurried Child: Growing Up Too Fast Too Soon*. New York: Alfred A. Knopf, 1985.

—— *Miseducation: Preschoolers at Risk*. New York: Alfred A. Knopf, 1987.

Faber, A. and E. Mazlish. *Liberated Parents/Liberated Children*. New York: Avon Books, 1974.

—— *How to Talk So Kids Will Listen & Listen So Kids Will Talk*. New York: Avon Books, 1980.

—— *Siblings Without Rivalry*. New York: W. W. Norton, 1987.

SUGGESTED READING LIST

Fraiberg, S. *The Magic Years: Understanding & Handling the Problems of Early Childhood.* New York: Charles Scribner's Sons, 1959.

Galinsky, E. *Between Generations.* New York: Berkely Books, 1981.

Galinsky, E., and J. David. *The Preschool Years.* New York: Times Books, 1988.

Gardner, R. *The Boys and Girls Book About Divorce.* New York: Bantam Books, 1981.

——— *The Boys and Girls Book About One-Parent Families.* New York: Bantam Books, 1983.

Ginott, H. G. *Between Parent & Child.* New York: Avon Books, 1956.

——— *Between Parents and Teenagers.* New York: Macmillan, 1969.

Glenn, H. S. and J. Nelsen. *Raising Self-Reliant Children in a Self-Indulgent World.* Fair Oaks: Sunrise Press, 1988.

Hochschild, A. *The Second Shift: Working Parents and the Revolution at Home.* New York: Viking, 1989.

Isaacs, S. *Who's In Control? A Parent's Guide to Discipline.* New York: Perigee Press, 1986.

Kaplan, L. J. *Oneness & Separateness: From Infants to Individuals.* New York: Simon & Schuster, 1978.

Lappé, F. M. *What to Do After You Turn Off the T.V.* New York: Ballantine Books, 1985.

Lerman, S. *Parent Awareness: Positive Parenting for the 1980's.* Minneapolis: Winston Press, 1981.

LeShan, E. *When Your Children Drive You Crazy.* New York: St. Martin's Press, 1985.

Miller, A. *Prisoners of Childhood: How Narcissistic Parents Form and Deform the Emotional Lives of their Gifted Children.* New York: Basic Books, 1981.

——— *For Your Own Good: Hidden Cruelty in Childrearing and the Roots of Violence.* New York: Farrar, Straus & Giroux, 1983.

Missildine, W. H. *Your Inner Child of the Past.* New York: Bantam Books, 1971.

Pearce, J. C. *Magical Child.* New York: Bantam Books, 1977.

——— *The Magical Child Matures.* New York: E. P. Dutton, 1985.

Peck, S. M. *The Road Less Traveled: A New Psychology of Love, Traditional Values and Spiritual Growth.* New York, Simon & Schuster, 1978.

Samlin, N. *Loving Your Child Is Not Enough: Positive Discipline that Works.* New York: Viking, 1987.

SUGGESTED READING LIST

Sanger, S. & J. Kelly. *The Woman Who Works, the Parent Who Cares.* New York: Little Brown & Company, 1987.

Satir, V. *Your Many Faces.* Millbrea, CA: Celestial Arts, 1978.

—— *The New Peoplemaking.* Palo Alto, CA: Science & Behavior Books, 1988.

Scott, L., and M. J. Angwin. *Time Out for Motherhood.* Los Angeles: Jeremy Tarcher, 1987.

Shreve, *A Remaking Motherhood: How Working Mothers are Reshaping Our Children's Future.* New York: Viking, 1987.

Trelease, J. *The Read-Aloud Handbook.* New York: Penguin Books, 1979.

Viorst, J. *Necessary Losses.* New York: Simon & Schuster, 1986.

Visher, J., and E. Visher. *Stepfamilies: A Guide to Working with Stepparents and Stepchildren.* New York: Bruner Mazel, 1979.

—— *How to Win as a Stepfamily.* Chicago: Contemporary Books, 1982.

Wallerstein, J. S., and S. Blakeslee. *Second Chances: Men, Women & Children a Decade After Divorce.* New York: Ticknor & Fields, 1989.

AUTHOR'S NOTE

I welcome any comments, questions, or suggestions you may have regarding the material I have presented in this book.

Stephanie Marston is available for lectures, conferences, workshops, and speaking engagements throughout the country. Please contact her at Raising Miracles Educational Seminars, 870 Galloway Street, Pacific Palisades, CA 90272.

INDEX

INDEX

rejection, saying "no" and, 53
respect:
  of limits, 49–51
  of privacy, 144–145
  self-, 25, 61–63
responsibility:
  authoritarian parenting and, 196
  children and, 177, 186–187, 200–201
  consequences and, 171, 173–174, 177
  defined, 171
  language of, 186–189
  problem-solving and, 186–187
  self-esteem and, 172
  showing of, 214–215
  when/then concept and, 226
ridicule, 135
risk taking, 121, 122
Road Less Traveled, The (Peck), 67
Rogers, Carl, 31
role models, 146–147, 233–234
Rosenthal, R., 114–115
rules:
  clarifying of, 189
  consequences and, 220–221
  democratic parenting and, 201
  house, 175, 176, 220
  personal, 220

Saint-Exupéry, Antoine de, 88
Samalin, Nancy, 107
sarcasm, 135, 160, 167
Satir, Virginia, 16–17, 20–21, 30, 49, 54
  prescription for touching by, 79
saying "no," 52–55, 199
scrapbooks (projects), 92
self-care inventory, 57–59
self-discipline, 176, 224
self-esteem, 17
  accepting feelings and, 135
  belonging and, 27, 28
  builders of, 60–64
  definition of, 24
  denial of feelings and, 133
  discipline and, 201–202
  encouragement and, 106–107
  factors for, 27
  freedom of expression and, 27, 30–31
  high, 26–27, 43–44
  inventory of, 45
  love and, 68
  low, 25–26, 37, 44
  lying and, 196
  parents and, 60–64
  photo project and, 92
  power and, 27, 29–30, 31
  responsibilities and, 172
  self-expression and, 63–64
  struggling and, 113–114
  success and, 119–120, 122–124
  touching and, 82
  uniqueness and, 27, 28–29
  verbal criticism and, 97–98
Self-Esteem in the Classroom (Canfield), 119
Self-Esteem Inventory (exercise), 45
self-motivation, 190–191
self-respect, 25, 61–63
self-sacrifice, 177–178
show-and-tell hour, 72
Showing Your Love (exercise), 95
single parents, 166
skin hunger, 80
smothering, mothering vs., 177–178
sounding board, 129–130
spanking, 197–198
"special guilt factor," 166
Spitz, René, 80
star chart, 214
Star for the Evening (exercise), 71–72
Strength Bombardment (exercise), 118–119
strengths, focusing on, 60–61
struggle muscle, 113, 179
success, 107, 119–120, 121, 122–124
supermother, 51–52
superparent syndrome, 48
Super Praise, 110–111
support groups, 236–237
Switch to the Positive (exercise), 125–126

taking risks, 121, 122
talking stick tradition, 94
talking together, 75–77
teaching:
  fun and, 184
  opportunities for, 184
  time for, 181–183, 186
  tips for, 183–184
Teach Only Love (Jampolsky), 85
teenagers, 25, 85, 111
Teilhard de Chardin, Pierre, 15
temper tantrums, 131, 153, 155, 157–158, 200, 206
terms of endearment, 83–84
That Makes Me Mad (exercise), 169–170
thinking before acting, 206, 209–210
threats, 135
  idle, 208
time, 68–72
  focused, 71, 213